THE ENTERTAINMENT WEEKLY *SEINFELD* COMPANION

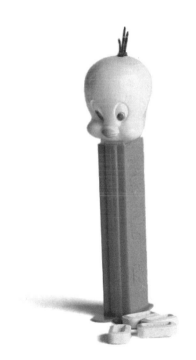

THE Entertainment WEEKLY

SEINFELD COMPANION

ATOMIC WEDGIES TO ZIPPER JOBS:

AN UNOFFICIAL GUIDE

TO TV'S FUNNIEST SHOW

BY BRUCE FRETTS

With an introduction by Lisa Schwarzbaum

Edited by Jeannie Park

WARNER BOOKS

A Time Warner Company

Copyright © 1993
by Entertainment Weekly Inc.
All rights reserved.

 **WARNER BOOKS**

A Time Warner Company

1271 Avenue of the Americas,
New York, NY 10020

Printed in the United States of America

First Printing: October 1993

10 9 8 7 6

ISBN: 0-446-67036-7
LC: 93-72548

BOOK DESIGN by
Michael Grossman and Bobby B. Lawhorn Jr.

COVER photographed for *EW* by Bonnie Schiffman/Onyx
BACK COVER photographed for *EW* by Gregory Heisler
STILL LIFE photographs by Anthony Verde

PAGE 12: Gino Mifsud
PAGE 14: Jan Sonnenmair
PAGE 16: Spike Nannarello
PAGE 23: Bettmann
PAGE 24: Photograph by Bonnie Schiffman/Onyx
PAGE 25: Paul Drinkwater
PAGE 26: Globe Photos
PAGE 31: Photograph by Bonnie Schiffman/Onyx
PAGE 33: Terry Smith
PAGE 34: Photofest
PAGE 36: Photofest
PAGE 37: Emilio Lari
PAGE 39: Bettmann
PAGE 44: Bettmann
PAGE 45: Murray Close
PAGE 46: Eddie Adams
PAGE 48: Jacques Haillot/Globe Photos
PAGE 49: Photograph by Bonnie Schiffman/Onyx
PAGE 50: Greg Schwartz
PAGE 51: Bettmann
PAGE 53: Walter Zurlinden/Globe Photos
PAGE 54: UPI, Globe Photos
PAGE 56: Bob Greene
PAGE 58: Greg Schwartz/Photofest
PAGE 64: Globe Photos
PAGE 67: Jane Bown/Globe Photos
PAGE 68: Photograph by Bonnie Schiffman/Onyx
PAGE 70: Bettmann
PAGE 74: Michael Yarish
PAGE 77: Globe Photos
PAGE 79: Paul Drinkwater
PAGE 80: Ted Horowitz/The Stock Market
PAGE 83: Wayne Williams
PAGE 85: Alice S. Hall
PAGE 88: Carin Baer
PAGE 91: Photofest
PAGE 92: McCliment/Silver
PAGE 95: Chris Haston
Tweety character TM & © Warner Bros. 1993. Used under license by Pez Candy, Inc.

To
M. E. H.

ACKNOWLEDGMENTS:

Thanks to the following ENTERTAINMENT WEEKLY staffers: Beth Arky, Alice H. Babcock, Martha K. Babcock, Sue Barnett, Ray Battaglino, George L. Beke, Annabel Bentley, Robin Bierstedt, Paul Bodley Jr., Gerald Burke, Joanne Camas, Kevin Christian, Evan J. Dong, Stacie Fenster, Alison Gwinn, Susan Isaak, Robert Kanell, Robert D. Kennedy, Bill Lazzarotti, Carlos Lema, Mary Makarushka, Carol A. Mazzarella, Steven Moonitz, Donald Morrison, Lisa DiSapio Motti, David Nagler, Sean O'Heir, Tom Roemlein, Michael T. Rose, Rachel Sapienza, B.J. Sigesmund, Marlena Sonn, Daneet Steffens, Daniel C. Thompson, and Ken Tucker.

Special thanks to Barbara Denler, Ann Finnegan, Steve Freeman, Brian Healy, Irv Kagan, Larry Karpen, Deneen Kelleghan, Karen Kelly, Jill Neal, Jose Romano, and Bob Warznak.

CONTENTS

INTRODUCTION

SOMETHING ABOUT NOTHING

FANS OF *SEINFELD* have mysterious ways of finding each other. "*Mulva!*" one stranger might exclaim to another. "*Snapple!*" "*These pretzels are making me thirsty!*" This is, of course, coded communication, a quizzing of sitcom sensibilities. It might as well be a measure of worldviews, a cultural litmus test. Because true *Seinfeld* enthusiasts know that appropriate responses include "*Delores!*" "*Junior Mints!*" "*Not that there's anything wrong with that!*"

And everybody else is off watching *Coach*.

The *Seinfeld* devotee appreciates that no other sitcom in television history has made such inventive, idiosyncratic use of words, labels, brand names, and pop-culture references. No other TV comedy has experimented as daringly with the witty possibilities of language on a medium that traditionally relies heavily on physical action for easy laughs. On *Seinfeld*, open-ended conversation among characters who have nothing to gain in terms of plot development is its own reward.

Is it any wonder that *Seinfeld* took so long to catch on?

Now that the show is widely regarded as network television's most innovative sitcom and its offbeat cast members have become full-fledged celebrities whose faces sell hair-care products and credit cards, one can easily forget that the show did not get off to a robust start when it premiered on NBC, first as an inauspicious one-shot in 1989, then as a five-episode series (which included a repeat of the pilot) in the summer of 1990. The stories hinged on the underachiever lives of then–36-year-old stand-up comedian Jerry Seinfeld and three fictional friends in Manhattan, and the idea was to show how the little observed details of daily urban living wove their way into Jerry's stand-up monologues, which punctuate each episode. With this premise, so low-key as to be nearly motionless, ratings were underwhelming (it was, don't forget, the summer). But a core population of viewers (and network executives) loved what they saw, and in the fall the series was renewed as a midseason replacement.

JERRY: His stand-up routines reflect the characters' everyday lives

Still, *Seinfeld* did not experience a rousing rebirth when it returned in January of 1991. Nor when it was jiggered from day to day, timeslot to timeslot, over the next two years. In fact, some 50 episodes came and went, during which time Jerry, ex-girlfriend Elaine Benes (Julia Louis-Dreyfus), best friend George Costanza (Jason Alexander), and apartment neighbor Kramer (Michael Richards) did nothing much of anything—hilariously. But meanwhile word of mouth spread, audience attachment grew, women began to pouf their hair like Elaine's sexy modified Gibson girl coif, and men placing personal ads in the classified sections of reputable journals began to list themselves as "Seinfeld look-alikes."

And then something remarkable happened: In February 1993, NBC shifted the show from Wednesday nights (where it had sulkily battled ABC ratings blockbuster *Home Improvement* for viewers) to Thursdays. And the small, vociferously devoted audience that had followed *Seinfeld* through six different schedule changes in four

years suddenly burgeoned into a large, vociferously devoted horde. The show immediately jumped from 40th place to 10th before settling confidently into the middle of the top 10 list. And the series officially became the comic phenomenon its supporters always knew it was.

FROM THE VERY BEGINNING, *Seinfeld* has attracted a passionately proprietary viewership—TV-literate, demographically desirable urbanites, for the most part— who look forward to each weekly episode in the Life of Jerry with a boomer generation's self-involved eagerness not seen since the height of *thirtysomething* in the '80s. To be a fan of *Seinfeld* is to join a cool club where bits of dialogue serve as secret passwords; to fully appreciate the show's unerringly neurotic heart is to understand that nothing on earth is as satisfying, as meaningful, as funny, or as important as sitting around with a couple of friends, wisecracking, squabbling, snacking, and otherwise putting off getting on with life.

ELAINE:
She's the only one of the four who works a regular job

Seinfeld makes sloth, lust, envy, and passive-aggression look like time well spent because, as the mantra now goes, *Seinfeld* is ostensibly about Nothing. As conceived by Jerry Seinfeld (who had logged 16 years on the road as a professional stand-up comic before the series was launched) and his friend and cocreator Larry David (whose own stand-up career was hampered in no small part by his propensity to berate the audience when they didn't laugh at his jokes), the sitcom is based on the tiniest air currents of cosmic disturbance—losing one's car in a parking lot, waiting in line for a movie, picking one's nose (or was it merely scratching?), eating chips with dip after the funeral of a girlfriend's aunt. These are the small-scale activities that fill one's time when one is not off, say, tending a bar in Boston where everybody knows your name or raising three kids on a blue-collar income in Lanford, Illinois.

But for a show that is ostensibly about nothing, *Seinfeld* has an astonishing lot go-

ing on: Jerry and George and Elaine and Kramer bet to see who can refrain the longest from masturbating. In one episode Jerry and George struggle to clarify a misperception that they are lovers; in another Jerry and George struggle to clarify a misperception that they are neo-Nazis. Kramer poses in his underwear for a Calvin Klein ad. Elaine inflames the passions of an NBC network executive, who goes off to work saving whales for Greenpeace in a doomed attempt to impress her. Jerry and George write a sitcom pilot for NBC—about "nothing," George explains with cocky pride. (Larry David, on whom the character of George is closely modeled, used the same description to pitch the real-life *Seinfeld* concept to real-life NBC executives.)

On *Seinfeld*, sitcom art has always imitated sitcom life, but the balance between the two has evolved. Indeed, as the characters have developed their own strong, interlaced identities, the structural emphasis has shifted: Now the stories are less

KRAMER: He dishes it out habitually with his friends at the corner diner

about how the comedian gets his material and more about the material itself—ordinary, minutia-rich daily life as Jerry, Elaine, George, and Kramer know it.

Besides, no stand-up routine could possibly do justice to how these people talk. And they do *talk*! Because it is based on character development rather than traditional sitcom action, *Seinfeld* is filled with great, quirky, quotable riffs and paradiddles of dialogue and free association. Brand names matter: Dockers jeans carry a specific resonance, as do Cuban cigars, Pez, and the memory of the late novelist John Cheever. Verbal one-upmanship counts, too (these are, after all, New Yorkers): If Jerry considers himself "Master of My Domain" for abstaining from masturbation, George is "King of the County" and Elaine is "Queen of the Castle." Opinions are confidently given; irritations are forcefully expressed. These people know one another, they borrow each other's clothing, they make free use of the food in Jerry's kitchen, they congregate at their local coffee shop to discuss what happened to them an hour earlier. They do not stand on sitcom ceremony. They take a load off, they hang out, they sit on Jerry's couch and turn their thoughts into *words*.

This is a novel sitcom idea.

AS *THE MARY TYLER MOORE SHOW* was the defining comedy of the '70s and *Cheers* marked the humor of the '80s, so *Seinfeld* signals the new age of the '90s, with conversation occupying the space that might otherwise be filled by life experience. Former lovers Jerry and Elaine are much more content to be neat friends than entangled romancers. George is much more comfortable complaining about being unemployed (as he usually is) than he is coping with the stresses of actually holding down a job (which he has done only occasionally, including a stint as a reader at the publishing company where Elaine, the only 9-to-5er in the bunch, works). Certainly Kramer has no apparent means of support, although he presumably made a bundle posing for Calvin Klein and would have

GEORGE:
He and Jerry write a sitcom pilot for NBC about "nothing"

made an even bigger bundle if Klein hadn't stolen his idea for a fragrance called The Beach and packaged it as a scent called Ocean.

All four friends are much happier once they are relieved of whatever romantic and sexual relationships they briefly find themselves in and can get back to the business of sitting around together, theoretically pursuing new romantic and sexual relationships. They have no children, they cook no meals, they belong to no bowling leagues, they own no amusingly run-down real estate, they don't care about interior decorating or home improvement or moving to Alaska.

So Jerry, George, Elaine, and Kramer have plenty of time to talk. Because talk is what gets them through life. It also makes *Seinfeld* the nimblest, most linguistically sophisticated comedy on the air today.

Which, of course, is why you need this book. Not that there's anything wrong with that. —*Lisa Schwarzbaum*

GLOSSARY

THIS, THAT, AND THE OTHER

AIR CONDITIONER:
Elaine is turned off
when it's not
turned on

Aggravation Installment Plan With Interest That Will Compound for Decades Prolonged guilt trip George says his parents will put him on if he shows up late for their 47th wedding anniversary dinner *(23*)*

Air Conditioner Convenience Jerry's mother refuses to use when Jerry and Elaine visit sweltering Florida *(20)*
◆ Kramer is carrying an unwieldy air conditioner when he loses his car in a New Jersey parking garage *(23)*
◆ Kramer suggests Newman try to beat a speeding ticket by saying he was racing to save the life of a suicidal Kramer, who was despondent because he had never owned an air conditioner *(42)*

The Airport Pickup/Drop-off The ultimate act of self-sacrificial loyalty—though it sometimes masks ulterior motives; Jerry is suspicious when George offers to pick him up at the airport during a blizzard *(15)*

◆ Elaine drives like a maniac to try to get an annoying beau on a plane back to Seattle *(17)*

◆ Jerry says he doesn't know baseball star Keith Hernandez well enough to drive him to the airport *(34)*

◆ George's car dies on the way to pick up Jerry at the airport, so they scam a free limo ride *(35)*

◆ Jerry and his father fight over who should pay for the gas after he picks up his parents *(43)*

◆ George's girlfriend Susan shows up late to the opera because she went to pick up a friend at the airport; by the time she arrives, George has already scalped one of their tickets *(47)*

◆ George has to pick up Jerry and Elaine after he loses a bet that he can jump high enough to touch the awning outside Jerry's building *(50)*

All Right, Sir Tom Snyderism Jerry and Elaine employ to indicate agreement or acceptance *(2, 3, 14)*

Amish Jerry's synonym for "grounded," indicating that, like the Pennsylvania Dutch people, the punished youngster is not allowed to drive, talk on the phone, or watch television—as in "You are Amish, young man, for the rest of this weekend!" *(42)*

LONI ANDERSON: Is she Jerry's dream date?

Loni Anderson Ex–*WKRP in Cincinnati* star who typifies the kind of woman Jerry's father thinks he should date—Jerry then tells George that the woman Jerry wants to ask out reminds him of Loni Anderson *(2)*

Anything What George doesn't feel he's doing if he watches a video at his own place—if he does it at Jerry's pad, he's doing something *(58)*

Apple Crunchy fruit that George consumes audibly while talking on the phone with women to make himself sound casual *(9)*
◆ Kramer eats apples whole, including the core, stem, and seeds *(15)*

Aquaman Half-man, half-fish comic book superhero whom Jerry thinks he saw on land a few times—George isn't sure Aquaman can survive outside water *(14)*

Ed Asner, Elijah Muhammad, and Secretariat Typically random group of famous figures who might be listed as sharing your birthday in a horoscope column—Jerry questions the usefulness of this information *(55)*

Atomic Wedgies Underwear torture in which the waistband is stretched up over the victim's head—George suffered it in high-school gym class on the orders of his teacher, Mr. Heyman*, who was fired for the offense. When George approaches a homeless Mr. Heyman 20 years later, he gets one again. *(22)*

APPLE: George's secret to good phone sex

B

¹**The Back** Section of clothing stores where salespeople go to try to find things that are never there—as Elaine puts it, "There's never anything good in the back; if they had anything good, they'd put it in the front." *(8)*

*Some character name spellings are phonetic

²The Back The part of the body that Elaine and Jerry's dad strain by sleeping on the same pull-out couch on separate occasions *(20, 43)*

◆ George offers to feign a back injury in order to delay a meeting with NBC *(48)*

◆ Mrs. Costanza hurts her back twice, first by keeling over when she walks in on George masturbating, and then by falling off the toilet when she reads an article alleging that her son is a homosexual *(49, 55)*

Backed Up Constipated condition Kramer endures after feeling a sudden urge to go to the bathroom during his *Jerry* audition but failing to find a rest room *(61)*

Baked Beans Canned legume Jerry and George remember their high-school gym teacher's rotten teeth resembling *(22)*

Bald Convention Conference an actress reading for the role of Elaine in *Jerry* says the lobby looks like when it is filled with actors trying out for the part of George *(61)*

Baldist Pejorative label George slaps on Elaine after she admits she has never dated a bald man *(25)*

Bald Paradise George's idyllic vision of what the 1930s must have been like in America, when all the men wore hats and none of the women could tell who had hair *(38)*

BAND-AID: Jerry's breakup tip— "One motion, right off!"

Banana Rapidly ripening fruit that Jerry often purchases despite the fact that it goes bad after one day *(58)*

Band-Aid Adhesive strip best removed in one quick motion; Jerry uses this process to illustrate the most painless way of splitting up with a woman *(6)*

The Beach Seaside scent Kramer dreams up after swimming with the Polar Bear Club and pitches to a Calvin Klein exec *(31)*
◆ Klein later introduces an identical fragrance called Ocean *(51)*

Because It's There The reason George claims he masturbates *(49)*

Beltless Trench Coat Ground-breaking men's outerwear fashion invented by Jerry's father in 1946 *(7)*

The Benes Tattoo Indelible imprint Jerry says Elaine puts on men with her charm *(17)*

BERLIN WALL:
Its toppling is
an all-purpose
alibi for Jerry

The Banker Story Alibi Kramer uses to try to help Newman overturn a speeding ticket; i.e., Newman was racing to save Kramer, who was going to commit suicide because he had never become a banker *(42)*

B.B.O. Abbreviation George coins for "Beyond Body Odor," applied to people exuding superhuman stenches; also known as "The Beast" *(59)*

Berlin Wall Cold War symbol Jerry uses as an excuse to avoid an obnoxious friend; i.e., he has choir practice for an evening of Eastern European national anthems to celebrate the Wall's fall *(4)*
◆ Jerry uses the Wall as an excuse to dump Marla the Virgin after he finds out she has a boyfriend; Jerry pretends he's going to Berlin, inspiring her boyfriend to go there for real, never to return *(48)*

ELAINE MARIE BENES

◆ a.k.a. Baby Doll *(35)*, Lainie *(55)*

◆ George's description of her: "Pretty woman, kind of short, big wall of hair, face like a frying pan" *(52)*

◆ Hails from Towson, Md., a suburb of Baltimore *(37)*

◆ Moved to New York City in 1985 *(21)*

◆ Works as a manuscript reader at Pendant Publishing *(8)*

◆ Says she had sex with Jerry 37 times when they were dating *(14)*

◆ Was appalled to receive $182 in cash as a birthday present from Jerry after they began dating again *(14)*

◆ Claims to have an IQ of 145, though her scores range from 85 to 151 *(24)*

◆ Once had the fleece torn out of her winter coat during a movie-theater seat-saving fracas *(52)*

◆ Is an anti-fur vegetarian who sometimes eats fish *(27)*

◆ Personality profile, courtesy of Jerry: She's "fascinated with Greenland," her favorite movie is *Shaft*, she likes talking during sex about current events and movies, she does a spiral thing with her tongue when she kisses *(61)*

Bermuda Triangle Paranormal phenomenon to which Jerry compares the chain reaction of phone calls from his uncle on Long Island to his parents in Florida to himself in Manhattan after Jerry insults his uncle—"It's like the Bermuda Triangle. Unfortunately, nobody ever disappears." *(16)*

Bermuda Triangle of Retail Cursed commercial property, like the site of Babu Bhatt's Dream Cafe, that suffers a constant turnover of failed businesses *(24)*

Corbin Bernsen *L.A. Law* star whom George bores backstage at *The Tonight Show* with a story about accidentally killing an ex-girlfriend's cat; Bernsen then ridicules George as a "sick nut" on the show *(40)*

Babu Bhatt Demonstrative Pakistani restaurateur Jerry befriends; Jerry's well-intended actions, however, cause Babu's business to fold and his visa to expire, and Babu swears revenge *(24, 53)*

Biff Teasing nickname Jerry gives George, a reference to Biff Loman in Arthur Miller's *Death of a Salesman*, "the biggest loser in the history of American literature" *(30, 31, 34, 53)*

Blindness Sightless condition Jerry feels would be distressing, primarily because he wouldn't know whether there were bugs in his food *(18)*

CORBIN BERNSEN: The *L.A. Law*yer hands down a judgment on George

◆ George guesses correctly that a violinist on the subway is faking blindness; he turns out to be an undercover cop who saves Kramer from being mugged *(30)*

◆ Newman claims to do charity work with blind people when he's on trial for speeding *(42)*

The Bold and the Beautiful Steamy soap opera Kramer lets himself into Jerry's apartment to watch *(3, 48)*

Bookman Tough-talking, no-nonsense library cop who busts Jerry for his long-overdue copy of *Tropic of Cancer (22)*

B.O. Squad Strike force Jerry thinks should be formed to roam the city washing down smelly people with brushes *(59)*

Botticelli Store where Elaine bought a high-priced pair of shoes that another of Jerry's ex-girlfriends covets *(54)*

Bouillabaisse Fish stew Kramer prepares when Jerry's parents come to visit *(2)*

◆ George says his cousin worked at a restaurant that used the pot of bouillabaisse as a toilet *(54)*

Bran Flakes Cereal Jerry claims to eat in a 25% variety: "The 40% was too much for me, so I found a store that would mix it up special" *(38)*

◆ Kramer orders 100% Bran Flakes when he's suffering from constipation *(61)*

Eva Braun Adolf Hitler's squeeze; an actress Kramer meets tells him about a miniseries she's developing

EVA BRAUN:
Is Hitler's honey worth a miniseries?

about Braun's life for German TV—"We know nothing about Eva Braun. What was it like having sex with Hitler?" *(40)*

Breakup by Association The transitive property through which George feels he can no longer be friends with Elaine because she and Jerry are no longer lovers *(14)*

The Bridge on the Starship Enterprise The male's quintessential living room, according to Jerry—a comfortable chair with a remote-control big-screen television *(10)*

Brother-and-Sister Couples People so perfect for each other they even look alike—George thinks he'll never be half of one of these couples because of the paucity of bald women *(34)*

The Bubble Boy Surly, plastic-tented adult fan of Jerry's to whom he, George, Susan, and Elaine pay a disastrous visit

BUTTON-FLY JEANS: Better safe than sorry, Jerry says

in upstate New York *(45)*
◆ The Bubble Boy watches *Jerry* with his parents and denounces the show as a "piece of crap" *(61)*

Bugs Bunny Rascally cartoon rabbit from whom Elaine says Jerry has gleaned all his knowledge of high culture *(47)*

Butler Profession of the comic character Jerry and George create for their NBC sitcom; in the script, a judge sentences an uninsured driver who crashed into Jerry's car to be Jerry's manservant *(48, 54, 61)*
◆ George has to be his father's butler after he damages the family car *(60)*

Button-Fly Jeans Style of denim pants George thinks may cause kidney problems but Jerry likes—"That is one place... where I do not need sharp, interlocking metal teeth" *(37)*

C

Cake Dessert Jerry warns he can't offer to a date who wants to come up to his apartment *(9)*
◆ Jerry upsets Elaine's roommate by eating the last piece of cake in the fridge *(14)*

Calling It Childhood law Jerry cites by which one can lay claim to the front seat of a car *(3)*
◆ George calls the window seat when he and Jerry fly to L.A. *(40)*

Can't Stand Ya George's sadistic high-school gym teacher's deliberate mispronunciation of his last name, Costanza *(22)*

Capillaries Tiny blood vessels around Jerry's eyes that burst when he goes scuba diving in Florida, making him look as if he has a pair of shiners *(20)*

JOHN CHEEVER: "Dear Henry, Last night with you was bliss..."

Cartwright A Chinese restaurant maître d's mangling of "Costanza"; George doesn't respond to this name and misses a vital phone call *(16)*

Cashmere Supersoft, extra-expensive wool that everyone loves; George buys Elaine a cashmere sweater for Christmas hoping she won't realize that it was marked down because of a tiny imperfection *(29)*

Cereal Famine Imaginary historical catastrophe Jerry gives as the reason for his family's immigration to America when he poses as Dubliner Dylan Murphy to commandeer a limo *(35)*

Neville Chamberlain Pushover World War II British Prime Minister whom Jerry and George revile: "Chamberlain! You could hold his head in the toilet [and] he'd still give you half of Europe." *(42)*

Chambermaids/Cleaning Women Workers toward whom Jerry and George admit an attraction; George has sex with one on his desk and loses his job at Pendant Publishing *(29)*
◆ Lupe, an L.A. hotel chambermaid, throws away a napkin on which Jerry has jotted down several precisely phrased jokes *(40)*
◆ George says the chambermaids work naked at nudist colonies *(49)*

Chapter Two Neil Simon play/movie from which an artist

girlfriend of Jerry's plagiarizes a heartrending monologue to use as a love letter to him *(37)*

John Cheever Bisexual novelist whose affair with Susan's father is revealed after a cache of love letters is recovered from the ashes of the family cabin *(46)*

CHERRY BINACA: Elaine's secret weapon against Crazy Joe Davola

CONCENTRATED Breath Spray

Binaca

NET WT 0.2 OZ (5.6g)

Cherish the Cabin The last words Susan's grandfather said to her father; the grandfather built the cabin in 1947, and Kramer burns it down with a cigar *(46)*

Cherry Binaca Fruit-flavored breath freshener Elaine sprays in Crazy Joe Davola's face after she stops by his apartment and discovers his psychopathic shrine to her *(47)*

Chess Match Fierce competition between Jerry's penis and his brain when he dates a vapid aspiring actress who titillates him physically but revolts him mentally *(26)*

Chocolate Syrup Gooey dessert topping that a performance artist George once dated threw on him from the stage, ruining his shirt and instigating a long-lived grudge *(15)*

A Chorus Line Musical Elaine's waitress/actress roommate auditions for, causing her to sing "God, I hope I get it!" around the apartment to Elaine's distraction *(3)*

Chucker A basketball player who shoots poorly and often; Jerry, Kramer, and Keith Hernandez call George a chucker, and finally George admits it *(34)*

Chuckles Five-flavored jelly candy that causes a brawl between two members of an ambulance crew taking George to the hospital after he has a reaction to holistic medicine *(13)*

La Cocina Off-Off-Broadway comedy about a Mexican chef that George claims he wrote when NBC execs ask him for his credentials; he says a moving company lost all the copies of the script *(42)*

Coffee Hot beverage that sometimes serves as a code word for "sex"—a date asks George up to her apartment for coffee, and George declines before figuring out what she really means *(9)*
◆ Lt. Bookman is amazed that Jerry doesn't keep coffee in his apartment *(22)*
◆ Kramer spills coffee on the IQ test Elaine is taking for George *(24)*
◆ Jerry asks a cop to escort him out of Monk's past Crazy Joe Davola, but the cop orders coffee, prolonging the agony *(42)*
◆ Jerry keeps only instant coffee in his kitchen—he gets his real coffee "on the outside" *(49)*

Colt 45 Malt liquor enjoyed by Kramer's booze-swilling ma, Babs *(26)*

CHUCKLES: A candy so good it's worth fighting for

GEORGE LOUIS COSTANZA

◆ a.k.a. Boy George *(21)*, Georgie Boy *(39)*, Georgie Porgie *(29)*, George Bonanza *(44)*, Costanza, Lord of the Idiots *(10)*

◆ Is right-handed, so he must sit on a woman's right side on a couch in order to make a move *(57)*

◆ Met Jerry at JFK High School when he fell off a rope in gym class and landed on Jerry's head *(55)*

◆ Among George's hidden talents, according to Jerry: He can "run like the wind," hoist 100 pounds over his head, and masterfully bait a hook *(33)*

◆ Jobs George thinks he might enjoy but for which he isn't qualified: general manager of a baseball team, color man for baseball telecasts, projectionist, talk show host, Civil War history professor, stable boy *(12)*

◆ Is proud of his "unblanched record of staunch heterosexuality" *(8)*

◆ Boasts of his formidable parallel parking abilities and comes from a family that regards paying for parking as the moral equivalent of patronizing a prostitute *(38)*

◆ Doesn't want to die with dignity; he has lived his whole life in shame, why should things change when he dies? *(61)*

Coma Etiquette Behavioral code Kramer tells Jerry doesn't exist; Kramer gives coma victims 24 hours to regain consciousness, then loots their belongings *(32)*

Come On Up Jerry's instructions to people who buzz his apartment from the lobby *(3, 6, 8, 19, 24, 25, 28, 29, 31, 32, 34, 36, 37, 42, 43, 44, 46, 47, 48, 49, 51, 53, 55, 56, 58, 60, 61)*

Compact Jeans Small-size denim pants (akin to compact cars), which only people with small rear ends should be allowed to wear, Jerry says *(38)*

Concentric Circles Expanding geometric pattern George drives in when hunting for a parking spot near Jerry's building *(38)*

Consolation Guy Social role George plays while accompanying a woman he is dating to a family funeral; Kramer says fulfilling this function equals 10 normal dates, and Jerry says it gives "instant boyfriend status" *(57)*

Cookies Baked goods Jerry consumes at will now that he's an adult and can ruin his appetite whenever he wants *(13)*
◆ Elaine criticizes Jerry's fructose-sweetened "health cookies" *(16)*
◆ Elaine and Jerry try to revive her elderly boyfriend by force-feeding him a cookie after he has a stroke while Elaine is trying to break up with him *(28)*
◆ Elaine raises a stink when she finds out first-class airline passengers are served cookies while people in coach aren't *(50)*

Cousin Jeffrey Never-seen relative of Jerry's whom Uncle Leo brags about; Cousin Jeffrey organized the New York City Parks

COOKIES: Elaine disdains the "dustboard fructose" taste of Jerry's snacks

THE GOOD FOR YOU COOKIE

RW Frookie®

ALL NATURAL

NEW!

FROOKWICH™

SANDWICH COOKIES

VANILLA

LOW IN SATURATED FAT

NO CHOLESTEROL

SWEETENED WITH FRUIT JUICE & FRUCTOSE

NET WT. 7.25oz./205g

Department's edible foliage tours *(7)*
◆ Uncle Leo thinks Jeffrey should write jokes for Jerry *(20)*

The Covenant of the Keys Unspoken contract by which a person who accepts a friend's spare keys agrees to use them only in the event of an emergency; Kramer breaks the covenant by perpetually letting himself into Jerry's apartment *(39)*

Crop Circles Unexplained British agricultural phenomenon that Jerry claims responsibility for in an attempt to impress a sexy woman he meets on an elevator *(26)*

Cuban Cigars Banned-in-the-USA stogies smoked by Fidel Castro and given as a gift from Susan's father to George, who finds them nauseating and passes them on to Kramer *(43)*
◆ Kramer sets Elaine's psychiatrist's Kleenex box on fire while trying to light one *(44)*
◆ Kramer starts trading Cubans for

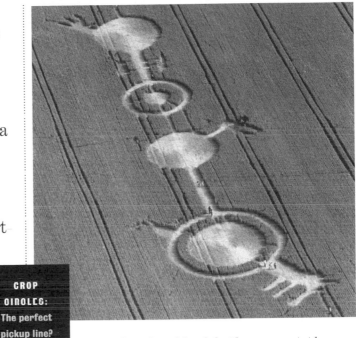

CROP CIRCLES: The perfect pickup line?

rounds of golf with the pro at the Westchester Country Club, and burns down Susan's father's cabin with one *(45)*
◆ Kramer runs out of the cigars and swaps his prized jacket to Cuban government officials for more *(46)*

Culottes Skirtlike short pants Jerry's mother bought for him in the girls' department when he was 5 years old; when Jerry is "outed," his father thinks the culottes caused his son to become a homosexual *(55)*

D

The *Daily News* New York City tabloid newspaper that George says is his only reason for getting up in the morning *(39)*

Ted Danson *Cheers* star whose astronomical per-episode salary George quotes repeatedly during his failed campaign to get NBC to up its $13,000 offer for *Jerry (42, 43, 44)*

TED DANSON: What's he got that George hasn't got?

Dark and Disturbed Qualities Jerry fakes in front of Cheryl Fong so that his sense of humor won't overshadow George's; nevertheless, Cheryl becomes attracted to the morose Jerry *(53)*
◆ Cheryl watches *Jerry* and then tells Ping, "I thought he was dark and disturbed" *(61)*

Dating Decathalon Herculean 72-hour relationship event George warns Jerry not to attempt when Jerry asks a new girlfriend to spend a weekend with him in Vermont *(5)*

Crazy Joe Davola Chemically unbalanced writer with vendettas against Kramer (for not inviting him to a party) and Jerry (for allegedly quashing his NBC deal) *(42)*
◆ Joe kicks Kramer in the head *(42)*
◆ Joe meets and falls for Elaine outside their shared shrink's office *(44)*
◆ Joe stalks Elaine when she goes to the opera with Jerry, George, and Kramer *(47)*

◆ Joe tries to ambush Jerry during the taping of his NBC pilot *(61)*

Joe DiMaggio New York Yankee great Kramer insists he saw dipping a donut in his coffee at Dinky Donuts; Jerry, Elaine, and George don't believe Kramer until they see DiMaggio dunk one with their own eyes *(18)*
◆ The DiMaggio dunking incident is immortalized in a speech the Kramer character delivers in *Jerry (61)*

Dockers Levi's pants with irritating TV ads that Jerry can't believe a girlfriend likes; he tells George and Kramer about it, and when they repeat it to her, she walks out on Jerry *(9)*

Do Me a Solid Kramerese for "Do me a big favor," as when he asks Jerry to sit in a double-parked car while he goes to a magician's pad to pick up doves *(8)*

Double Crunch Cereal found on Jerry's well-stocked kitchen shelf *(32, 51)*

Double Dipping Social faux pas of sticking a chip back into the dip after taking a bite; George double dips at a funeral, setting off a melee *(57)*
◆ Backstage at *Jerry*, George continues his double dipping ways *(61)*

The Drake and the Drakette Nicknames for Scott Drake (a friend of Jerry's whom Elaine and Kramer also like, but George hates) and his fickle fiancée, Allison; when they call off their engagement and refuse to return gifts, the gang decide they hate the Drake and the Drakette *(60)*
◆ While watching *Jerry*, the Drake says he loves "the Sein," but the Drakette says she hates "the Sein" *(61)*

Drake's Coffee Cake Crumb-covered snack that Jerry uses to bribe Newman not to tell his neighbor

DRAKE'S COFFEE CAKE: It's not big enough to keep Newman's mouth shut

Martín that Jerry dated his girlfriend when Martín was in a coma *(32)*

The Dreaded Apparatus Kramer's euphemism for an enema, which he purchases to relieve constipation; also known as "The Big E" and "Wet and Wild" *(61)*

Dream Cafe Food spot opened by Babu Bhatt serving such diverse dishes as tacos, moussaka, franks and beans, turkey, and rigatoni; Jerry convinces Babu to introduce an all-Pakistani menu, and the café soon goes bankrupt *(24)*

Dream Spot George's favorite parking place, directly across the street from Jerry's building and right in front of Tom's Market and Almo's Bar & Grill *(38)*

The Elephant Man Grotesquely disfigured 19th-century Englishman to whom Elaine compares Kramer's ex-girlfriend's personality *(21)*
◆ Jerry suggests George needs a team of psychiatrists equal to the number of doctors who studied the Elephant Man *(42)*
◆ After being falsely branded a nosepicker, Jerry invokes a line from the 1980 biopic *The Elephant Man*: "I am not an animal!" *(51)*

Elmer Fudd Sitting on a Juicer Lisping cartoon character perched on a kitchen appliance which Jerry tells George a

THE ELEPHANT MAN: Picked-on Jerry quotes John Hurt's character

date's grating laugh sounds like; when she overhears George repeat this description, she ditches Jerry *(45)*

The Enthusiastic "Hi!" Extra-excited phone greeting George requires from potential girlfriends *(9)*

Epstein–Barr With a Twist of Lyme Disease Dual disorder Elaine's chronically fatigued waitress/actress roommate contracts; Elaine thinks her roomie caught Lyme disease from a tick while performing in an outdoor production of *Hair* *(15)*

Every Time I Think I'm Out They Pull Me Back In Al Pacino line from *The Godfather Part III*, which George paraphrases when he realizes he can't break up with Susan as soon as he would like *(48)*

Excuse Rolodex Quick-reference list Jerry keeps near his telephone to provide a handy supply of false reasons ("waiting for the cable man…ran out of underwear") that he can't see a self-centered friend *(4)*

EVERY TIME I THINK I'M OUT…: Girlfriends sometimes make George feel like Al Pacino

Eyebrows Facial feature Jerry says office workers raise in lieu of saying hello to coworkers the second time they see them in a given day *(12)*

◆ Elaine's elderly beau has overgrown eyebrows, but she can't bring herself to tell him to trim them *(28)*

◆ Elaine says women put themselves through physical pain to groom their eyebrows, but Jerry and George don't care about women's eyebrows *(33)*

F

Face-to-Face Breakup In-person severance Jerry tells Elaine she must perform after a certain point in a relationship: "Seven dates is a face-to-face breakup" *(28)*

Farfel Obnoxious dog left in Jerry's care by a drunken airplane seat-mate *(21)*

Flaming Globes of Sigmund Dialogue snippet Jerry writes down as a possible punch line while nodding off in front of a sci-fi movie; the next day, he can't read his note, and others interpret it as "Fax me some halibut," "Don't mess with Johnny," "Salami salami baloney," and "Cleveland 117, San Antonio 109" *(13)*

Flea Market Open-air bazaar where Kramer purchases five Pez dispensers; George admits he doesn't know what a flea market is, but he thinks fleas are somehow involved *(31)*
◆ George and Elaine borrow Jerry's car to go to a flea market, and George hits a pothole when Elaine adjusts the rearview mirror to check out the shades she bought *(38)*

REDD FOXX: George can match him word for word

Flip a Coin Random method Jerry and George use to determine who will get an apartment they both want; Jerry wins, but George calls interference because the coin hit the table *(3)*
◆ George guesses the couple flip a coin to decide who's the bride and who's the groom at a lesbian wedding *(30)*

Cheryl Fong Attorney George dates briefly; she persuades her cousin Ping to drop his lawsuit against

MAHATMA GANDHI: "He used to dip his bald head in oil..."

Freaks Kramer's surefire concept for Jerry and George's NBC sitcom: "Who wouldn't tune in to see a woman with a mustache? The tallest man in the world? A guy who's just a head?" *(42)*

Friends-in-Law Elaine's term for her relationship with George because they can interact only through Jerry *(21)*

The Full Turn With the Eye Roll

The most drastic step Jerry can take against talkers behind him in a movie without inciting a fistfight *(5)*

G

Elaine but changes her mind when she finds out how dark and disturbed George really is; also known as "The Terminator" *(53)*
◆ Cheryl watches *Jerry* with Ping *(61)*

Harry Fong Fake name George makes up for the portly stranger to whom he scalps an opera ticket *(47)*

Redd Foxx Foul-mouthed comic Jerry compares George to when telling the story of George's infamous "curse toast" at a friend's wedding *(47)*

Mahatma Gandhi Frequently fasting Hindu leader Elaine compares herself to while ravenously waiting for a table at a Chinese restaurant *(16)*
◆ Elaine isn't allowed to eat for three days before taking an ulcer test, and

Jerry tells her about the Mahatma's prefast snack habits: "Gandhi loved Triscuits" *(32)*

◆ Elaine befriends an old woman who says she had an affair with Gandhi: "He used to dip his bald head in oil and rub it all over my body" *(56)*

Gatorade Thirst-quenching beverage that Kramer once persuaded a stand-up comic to pour on a nightclub owner's head after a softball game, causing the club owner to die of pneumonia and the comic to become a drug addict *(31)*

Get Out! Elaine's expression of extreme disbelief, which she accompanies with a hard shove to the person's chest; "Shut up!" is a variation *(10, 43, 58)*

Get Outta Here! Phrase George is upset his doctor didn't use to answer the question "Is it cancer?" *(61)*

GLAMOUR

WILL YOUR LOVE LAST? 8 early clues

FALL FASHION NEWS

TRICKS TO CUT YOUR BEAUTY TIME

GLAMOUR: George's mom never should have left it lying around

Get-Out-of-Relationship-Free Cards Monopoly-like passes Jerry thinks people should be able to use to extricate themselves from romantic entanglements; can be overridden only by an "Eight More Months of Guilt, Torture, and Pain Card" *(48)*

Get Up Early Getaway alibi Elaine says men always use after sex: "They all turn into farmers suddenly" *(48)*

◆ Elaine's boyfriend uses it after she absorbs B.O. from Jerry's car *(59)*

Glamour Women's magazine George was flipping through when he felt the irresistible desire to masturbate in his parents' house *(49)*

Gloves Articles of clothing Kramer left in Jerry's car when it was stolen; Jerry calls the thief on his car phone, and Kramer asks him to return the gloves, which he does *(28)*

◆ Kramer raids a hospital supply closet for the proper gloves to wear while redoing his apartment in wood *(58)*

Goiter Football-shaped protuberance on the neck of an aged woman Elaine volunteers to visit; Elaine can't look at it—"I keep thinking that goiter's gonna start talking to me" *(56)*

Goldfish Fragile underwater pets Elaine totes around while she, Jerry, George, and Kramer search for Kramer's car in a mall parking garage *(23)*

Good Meeting Story Amusing anecdote that all successful couples have about their first encounter; George thinks he has never had a lasting relationship because he never meets women in interesting ways *(36)*

The Good Ones Desirable men who are in such demand that they refuse to commit to one woman; Elaine says Jerry thinks he's one of The Good Ones *(33)*

The Good Spot in Front of the Good Building in the Good Neighborhood George's father's ideal parking space; George knows he won't be allowed to borrow the family car if his father has managed to park it there *(60)*

GOLDFISH: How long can they survive in a sealed bag?

Greenpeace Environmental group NBC president Russell Dalrymple joins after Elaine spurns him because she doesn't respect his work *(61)*

Guys and Dolls Lavish Broadway musical George buys Jerry two tickets to see for his birthday; after they are "outed," Jerry doesn't want to go with George *(55)*

Gymnastics Coach Job George thinks Jerry's character should have in his sitcom; when Jerry rejects this idea, George suggests antiques-shop owner instead *(42)*

H

Had To and Maybe Verbal cues given by a sexually uninterested woman, according to George: "She said she '*had to* come into town…and *maybe* we'd get together?' …You're not going to see this woman" *(1)*

Hand Synonym for control in a relationship, taken from the phrase "the upper hand"; a vital goal for George—"A man without hand is not a man" *(31)*

Hand Sandwich A two-handed, top-and-bottom handshake George considers an unclear signal of a woman's intentions *(1)*

Mary Hart Cheery *Entertainment*

MARY HART:
What is it about her voice that drives Kramer crazy?

Tonight anchor whose voice causes convulsions in Kramer *(36)*

Havana Rented Robert Redford movie Jerry lends to Elaine, who keeps it for two weeks, costing Jerry $35 *(48)*

Headfirst Parking Parallel parking technique that is anathema to George, who clashes with a driver pulling forward into a space into which George is backing *(38)*

Healthy Adulthood Stage of life that George feels he has missed after he thinks he has had a heart attack: "I haven't outgrown the problems of puberty, [and] I'm already facing the problems of old age" *(13)*

Hennigans Brand of scotch that doesn't cause the drinker to emit an odor—Kramer calls it the "no-smell, no-tell scotch"; Jerry says it also works as a paint thinner; George uses it to

EVANDER HOLYFIELD: He's more than a champ in George's eyes

Hezbollah Radical Muslim fundamentalist group Jerry claims invited him to Iran to perform; actually, he's testing a self-involved friend's listening skills *(4)*

Evander Holyfield Boxer whose picture George is mesmerized by while in the midst of a panic about his sexuality *(18)*

Home Alone Movie Elaine points to as an example of how people forget things when she is trying to convince Kramer it slipped her mind to invite him to a flea market *(38)*
◆ George watches *Home Alone* on Jerry's VCR; George hated the sequel but thinks that was because he hadn't seen the original *(58)*

Home Base Kramer's term for his toilet, which he stays near while he's constipated in case he receives any "news from the front" *(61)*

Home-Bed Advantage Favorable situation with overnight female guests that Jerry thinks he may lose if Elaine moves into

seduce a cleaning woman *(29)*
◆ Elaine downs a large glass of Hennigans before concocting a cockamamy explanation of how she and George damaged Jerry's car *(38)*

Keith Hernandez Ex–New York Met first baseman whom Jerry befriends, Elaine briefly dates, and Kramer and Newman wrongly accuse of spitting on them *(34)*

his building and constantly drops by his place *(10)*

L. Ron Hubbard Deceased Scientologist leader and author of *Dianetics* of whom George speaks disdainfully, causing a Hubbard-ite to refuse to drive him around a parking garage searching for a lost car *(23)*

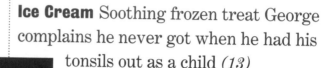

L. RON HUBBARD: You never know where you'll find one of his followers

Ice Cream Soothing frozen treat George complains he never got when he had his tonsils out as a child *(13)*
◆ An ice-cream truck can't get by when George fights with another driver over a parking space *(38)*

"If I Were a Rich Man" Jewish-themed *Fiddler on the Roof* tune George nervously whistles while posing as neo-Nazi leader Donald O'Brien *(35)*

Inka Dink Impartial method Jerry uses to decide whether Kramer or George gets a statue once owned by Jerry's grandfather *(11)*

I'm Gonna Rip Him a New One Proctological promise made by the director of *Jerry* after George keeps bothering him with suggestions *(61)*

INDIANA: George tips his hat to Harrison Ford's movie character

I'm Gonna Sew His Ass to His Face Threat leveled against George by the husband of a woman with whom George has had sex *(36)*

Impending Intestinal Requirement George's polite term for the feeling of on-coming flatulence; also known as an "un-stoppable force" *(16)*

Indiana Nickname Jerry gives George when he wears an Indiana Jones–style hat he bought at a flea market *(38)*

Invisible Coffee Table Transparent piece of furniture Kramer builds with a windshield he found; he gives it to his girlfriend (who is also Elaine's roommate), but they shatter it while making out on the floor *(19)*

It Moved George's reason for thinking he's gay after he gets a massage from a man; Jerry repeats a gym teacher's claim that someone is gay only if it moves because of direct contact *(18)*
◆ The incident is used as plot fodder for *Jerry (61)*

J

Jackets Seminal piece of clothing in the Seinfeld universe; Jerry's mother harangues his father for wearing an unsuitable jacket to a relative's anniversary party *(7)*
◆ Jerry buys a pricey suede jacket and stains it by wearing it in a snowstorm *(8)*
◆ Jerry asks a hospitalized George if he

PETER JENNINGS: A face too good to be true, George claims

zipper from a vacation he took six years earlier, because "women like skiers" *(48)*

◆ George makes a bad first impression on a therapist by struggling with his jacket zipper throughout his first session *(51)*

◆ Kramer spills mustard on Elaine's jacket when he sits in her seat at a movie theater *(52)*

◆ Elaine refuses to take her green parka off indoors, to everyone's annoyance *(55)*

◆ Kramer borrows Jerry's jacket for a date, not realizing it was infected with B.O. from Jerry's contaminated car *(59)*

can have George's treasured Blackhawks jacket if he dies *(13)*

◆ Jerry's parents remind him that when he was 14 he left his jacket on a bus *(23)*

◆ Babs Kramer's ex-boyfriend, Albert Pepper, forces Kramer to return a mythic, babe-attracting jacket Pepper left at Babs' house two years earlier *(24)*

◆ Kramer asks Elaine to pose as Pepper's daughter, Wanda, so he can get into Pepper's place and retrieve the jacket *(26)*

◆ Kramer trades the jacket for Cuban cigars *(46)*

◆ George keeps a lift ticket on his jacket

The James Bond of Laundry Title Jerry gives a Laundromat owner who claims no responsibility for clients' valuables, thus granting himself "a license to steal" *(12)*

Peter Jennings Anchorman who George claims had a nose job when he's trying to convince one of his girlfriends that she should get one *(26)*

Jerry Title of NBC sitcom pilot that Jerry and George cowrite based on their mundane lives; the title page of the script floats into the ocean after NBC president Russell Dalrymple falls overboard from a Greenpeace vessel *(61)*

Lyndon Johnson U.S. President whom Kramer tells a couple their baby daughter resembles *(34)*
◆ George's nominee for all-time ugliest world leader *(55)*

Mr. Johnson Jerry's name for Kramer's penis; after Kramer accidentally sees Elaine naked, Kramer offers to strip for her in Jerry's apartment, but Jerry warns him, "You're always welcome in my home, but as far as Mr. Johnson is concerned, that's another story" *(19)*

Junior Mint Refreshing chocolate candy Kramer

accidentally drops into a patient's sliced-open body from an operating theater balcony *(58)*

K

Kennedys Powerful political clan that Elaine claims to be unimpressed by, only to pester a friend who is married to a distant Kennedy relative with questions about Rose Kennedy and Sargent Shriver *(15)*
◆ Kramer and Newman's flashback to the Shea Stadium spitting incident is shot as a parody of the Oliver Stone movie *JFK (34)*
◆ When Kramer thinks George and Jerry are neo-Nazis, he becomes convinced they must know who killed John F. Kennedy *(35)*
◆ Elaine flirts with John F. Kennedy Jr. at her

JUNIOR MINTS: A medical miracle from above, courtesy of Kramer

Creamy mints in pure chocolate
Junior Mints
NET WT. 1.60 OZ.

health club, but he ends up deflowering Jerry's virgin girlfriend *(49)*

◆ JFK Jr. and the ex-Virgin watch *Jerry* in bed *(61)*

Ketchup Condiment Elaine is discussing with NBC president Russell Dalrymple when he peeks at her cleavage and falls madly in love with her *(54)*

The Keys Title of the movie treatment Kramer shops around L.A., inspired by his falling-out with Jerry over spare apartment keys *(40)*

The Kibosh Evil hex Crazy Joe Davola thinks Jerry put on Joe's NBC deal, and Joe now vows to put on Jerry; may also be used as a verb: "You know I've kiboshed before. And I'll kibosh again." *(47)*

The Ayatollah Khomeini Voraciously vengeful Iranian cleric whom Jerry thinks George rivals in ferocity of grudge-holding *(15)*

Calvin Klein Fashion designer and fragrance mogul whose company Kramer offers The Beach *(31)*

◆ Klein hires Kramer to model his line of men's jockey shorts in magazine ads *(51)*

◆ Klein watches *Jerry* and likes Seinfeld's style *(61)*

THE AYATOLLAH KHOMEINI: Don't get on his bad side—or George's

C. Everett Koop Crusading former surgeon general; Jerry thinks Elaine matches him in her disdain for cigarette smokers *(34)*

Kosher Meal Religiously correct airline food George reminds himself to order for his flight to L.A. *(40)*

◆ Elaine is served a kosher meal against her will *(50)*

Babs Kramer Kramer's never-seen, never-heard, hard-drinking, opera-loving mom *(26, 39)*

KRAMER

- a.k.a. The K-Man *(17)*, Krame *(27)*
- Ran away from home at 17 and jumped aboard a steamer for Sweden *(37)*
- Claims to have "dark brown eyes, like rich Colombian coffee" *(37)*
- Hates being called "hipster dufus" *(60)*
- An inveterate moocher who has asked to borrow these items from Jerry: meat *(1)*, salad dressing *(2)*, tea and a spatula *(3)*, ketchup *(4)*, mini-Ritz crackers *(8)*, cereal and a bowl *(26)*, a popcorn popper *(39)*, brown mustard and pickles *(41)*, calamine lotion *(43)*, Double Crunch cereal and a Dustbuster *(51)*
- Likes to take bubble baths *(39)*
- Always wanted to "drive [a] big rig" and thinks "nothing's sexier than a woman behind the wheel of a semi" *(39)*

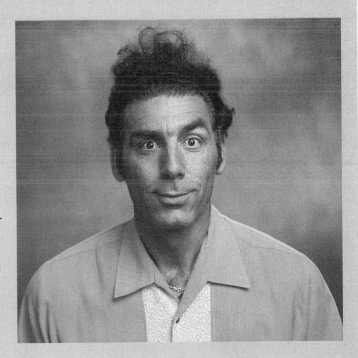

- Believes home package delivery should be outlawed because burglars pose as Federal Express employees *(43)*
- Does the worst Cockney accent Jerry has ever heard *(25)*
- Orders extra MSG with his Chinese food *(48)*
- Prefers to be on the bottom during sex *(61)*

Isosceles Kramer Name Kramer says he would like to give to his child, if he ever has one *(60)*

The Kramer Portrait of Kramer in his beloved jacket painted by an artist girlfriend of Jerry's and purchased by a pair of pretentious collectors. "His struggle is man's struggle…he's a loathsome, offensive brute, yet I can't look away." *(37)*

Kramerica Industries Company Kramer creates to open a chain of make-your-own-pizza restaurants *(4)*

THE KRAMER:
"He's a loathsome, offensive brute…"

L-Dopa Neurological medication Jerry tells a dull party guest he's taking to explain why he's patting himself on the head; he's actually sending a secret signal to Elaine to rescue him *(27)*

Leg Man Fetishistic label Jerry doesn't merit—he says he's a breast man: "Why would I be a leg man? I don't need legs" *(57)*

Lesbianism Sexual orientation to which George claims he has driven women *(19)*
◆ Elaine is selected to be the best man at a lesbian wedding *(30)*
◆ Jerry boasts that he can identify lesbians on sight: "I happen to have a very keen lesbian eye" *(57)*
◆ Susan dates a woman after breaking up with George, but Kramer steals Susan's lover *(59)*

different levels, with steps. It'll be carpeted. A lotta pillows. You know, like ancient Egypt." Jerry bets he won't finish the project in a year, and Kramer calls off the bet when he quits before ever starting *(7)*
◆ The levels discussion is later dramatized as a scene in *Jerry (61)*

Abe Lincoln and Mary Todd First Couple to whose tempestuous marriage Kramer compares Jerry and Elaine's stormy romantic relationship *(37)*

ABE LINCOLN AND MARY TODD: Jerry and Elaine, circa 1850

◆ Susan dates another one of George's ex-girlfriends *(61)*

David Letterman Late-night talk-show host on whom Susan has a crush, and for whom George hopes Susan will dump him; George says he approached Letterman about it at NBC and Letterman told him "next time [you] should probably break the Prozacs in half" *(48)*

Levels Kramer's radical design concept for his apartment—"I'm going to build these

The Little Man Omniscient inner voice Kramer says one must always heed; George won't listen because he says his "little man's an idiot" *(51)*

The Little Room Smaller, second waiting room in a doctor's office, which George loathes because he has to sit in it alone *(6)*

The Look Lustful gaze Jerry gives Elaine when he wants to have sex with her *(14)*
◆ Elaine gets the look in the pilot for *Jerry (61)*

Sophia Loren Sultry Italian actress Jerry's mom mentions when she thinks he's being too picky about women: "So who are you looking for, Sophia Loren?" *(2)*

Mike Lupica New York *Daily News* sports columnist whom George names as one of his favorite writers when trying to get a job at Pendant Publishing *(29)*

ELLE MACPHERSON: George's missed chance is Kramer's day in the sun

Lupus? Is It Lupus? Worst-case conclusion George jumps to when expecting bad news about his health *(13, 32)*

Yo Yo Ma Cellist whose name Kramer repeats incessantly after being kicked in the head by Crazy Joe Davola *(42)*

"MacArthur Park" Hit '60s single George says he was singing when he dropped and broke a cherished family statue he was using as a makeshift microphone *(11)*

Elle Macpherson *Sports Illustrated* swimsuit model with whom Kramer plays nude backgammon on a Cayman Islands trip George passed up on a psychic's advice *(32)*

Magic Loogie Warren Commission–esque term Jerry applies to the single gob of saliva Kramer and Newman claim struck them in four separate places *(34)*

The Male Code Set of rules by which men interact; e.g., if two men go to a party and one gets lucky, he is under no obligation to drive his friend home *(27)*

Jayne Mansfield Top-heavy actress Jerry mentions to Sidra, hoping she will tell him if she ever had her breasts enlarged *(57)*

Mickey Mantle New York Yankees legend whom Jerry and Kramer idolize; Jerry sarcastically guesses Mantle as the answer to Uncle Leo's question "Do you know who Cousin Jeffrey comes to when he has trouble with one of the big shots at the Parks Department?" *(7)* ◆ Kramer punches Mantle in the mouth during a bench-clearing brawl at a Florida fantasy camp; when Kramer grovels for forgiveness at Mantle's New York restaurant, he's tossed in the street *(53)* ◆ Jerry says that hearing Elaine say Sidra has fake breasts is "like finding out Mickey Mantle corked his bat" *(57)*

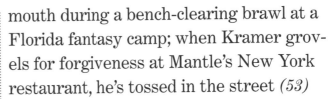

JAYNE MANSFIELD: She was all real, but is Sidra?

Master of the House Line from a *Les Misérables* song that gets stuck in George's head; he passes it on to Elaine's crabby father *(8)*

Master of Your Domain Title bestowed upon those who abstain from masturbation; George's variation is "King of the County," Jerry's is "Lord of the Manor," and Elaine's is "Queen of the Castle" *(49)*

The Master Packer Name Jerry gives himself by virtue of his ability to prepare a perfect suitcase *(3)*

Matador Bullfighting profession whose mystique George doesn't get: "I don't see the big deal.... You wave the cape, the bull charges, and you get out of the way." *(10)*

◆ Elaine claims she once dated a matador to impress a married couple who make her feel inadequate *(36)*

Maybe the Dingo Ate Your Baby Paraphrased line from the Meryl Streep movie *A Cry in the Dark* uttered by Elaine as a snide response to a party guest's cloying complaint, "I have lost my fiancé, the poor baby" *(27)*

Roger McDowell Ex–New York Mets relief pitcher revealed to be the actual spitter instead of Keith Hernandez; he expectorated on Kramer and Newman from the gravelly road behind the bushes outside Shea Stadium *(34)*

Golda Meir Former Israeli head of state whom Elaine names as all-time ugliest world leader; runners-up are Lyndon Johnson, Charles de Gaulle, and Leonid Brezhnev *(55)*

GOLDA MEIR: Elaine ranks the Israeli prime minister (upper left) over de Gaulle (lower left), Johnson (upper right), and Brezhnev in a face-off of world leaders

Sergio Mendes Brazilian bossa nova bandleader who Kramer says has such an enormous cult following, he "can't even go to the bathroom in South America!" *(56)*

Russ Meyer Breast-obsessed director to whose films Elaine compares Monk's Cafe after the owner starts hiring big-busted waitresses *(61)*

Mickey Tranquilizer George delightedly drops into his ex-boss's drink: "I'm going to slip him a Mickey....It's like a movie!" *(12)*

Bette Midler Flamboyant chanteuse beloved by gay audiences whom Jerry is ashamed to admit he likes after he is "outed" *(55)*

Milanos Chocolate-filled cookies a hungry George is tempted to swipe off the dashboard of an L.A. cop car *(41)*

Mint Floss Green-colored dental aid that drops from George's pocket during a date, destroying the romantic mood *(4)*

Monk's Cafe Coffee shop where Jerry, George, Elaine, and Kramer gather regularly to discuss their lives *(3, 4, 5, 6, 7, 9, 10, 11, 13, 14, 15, 19, 22, 25, 26, 28, 29, 30, 31, 34, 39, 40, 42, 45, 46, 48, 49, 51, 53, 54, 55, 56, 59, 61)*

Moom Misspelled tattoo Jerry joshingly claims he sued to have removed *(2)*

Moops Trivial Pursuit typo that incites a fistfight between George and the Bubble Boy; George says "Moops," not "Moors," is the correct answer to the question "Who invaded Spain in the 8th century?" *(45)*

Morning Mist George's name for the outfit he wears for his flight to L.A.—a plain brown baseball cap, green oxford shirt, blue pants, and sneakers (he picks his clothes based on his mood) *(40)*

Morning Thunder Tea that makes Jerry hyper; he doesn't know it contains caffeine, and Elaine won't tell him *(21)*

Moses Ten Commandments recipient who George is convinced must have been a nose-picker: "You walk through the desert for 40 years with that dry air, you're telling me you're not gonna have occasion to clean house a little?" *(51)*

MINT FLOSS: George should have left it at home

"The Most Beautiful Girl (in the World)" Woeful '70s country song that George sings when he starts missing Susan after their breakup *(51)*

The Most Beautiful Woman I've Ever Seen Crazy Joe Davola's elated description of Elaine to his psychiatrist, moments after meeting her in front of the doctor's office *(44)*

Johnson & Johnson
MINT
UNWAXED
DENTAL FLOSS

Mulva Jerry's guess at a date's name he can't recall—she mentions it rhymes with a female body part (other possibilities Jerry and George come up with are Celeste, Aretha, Bovary, Gipple, and Delores) *(58)*

Murphy Brown Candice Bergen sitcom for which Elaine tries to write a script; when Kramer runs off to L.A., he lands a guest spot as Steven Snell, Murphy Brown's newest assistant *(39)*
◆ Kramer calls the *Murphy Brown* set later and asks to speak to Bergen but gets hung up on *(40)*

MURPHY BROWN: Is Kramer the secretary she has been searching for?

[1]My Boys George's nickname for his sperm; when he thinks he has impregnated a woman, he rejoices, "My boys can swim!" *(33)*

[2]My Boys Jerry and Kramer's nickname for their genitals; Jerry resists lending Kramer his swimsuit because he doesn't want Kramer's boys "down there" *(57)*

My Guys Jerry's nickname for his clothes; he doesn't want to share a washing ma-chine with Kramer because he doesn't want his guys mixing with Kramer's guys *(12)*

Buck Naked George's chosen name for himself if he ever becomes a porno star *(49)*

The Naked Gun Gag-filled movie comedy Jerry refuses to watch with a date who has an irksome laugh; he suggests they watch the concentration-camp miniseries *Holocaust* instead *(45)*

The Naked Station All-nude cable network Jerry and Elaine land on while channel-surfing; George says he can't allow himself to get cable because "if I had that in my house, I'd never turn it off" *(14)*

Nathan's Hot Dog Brooklyn frank Jerry devours after riding the subway to Coney Island to recover his stolen car *(30)*

Ozzie Nelson Sweater-wearing TV father figure to whose sartorial stylings Jerry compares Kramer's square chic look *(47)*

Newman Unseen Kramer pal who threatens to commit suicide because he doesn't have a job or a girlfriend; he jumps from a second-story window and lies on the ground feigning injury *(12)*
◆ Newman makes his first appearance, saying he doesn't eat fruit because it makes him incontinent and doesn't go to the beach since he freckles *(32)*
◆ Jerry often greets him with a hostile "Hello, *Newman*" *(34, 39, 56)*
◆ Newman joins George in his stand against headfirst parking *(38)*
◆ Newman talks like a bad '40s movie: "He packed a grip and he split for the Coast. La La Land. El Lay." *(39)*
◆ Newman claims he had a girlfriend once, "and she was pretty wild!" *(42)*
◆ Newman immediately spots Elaine's nipple on her Christmas card *(51)*
◆ Newman works at the post office: "The mail keeps coming and coming...then, it's Publishers Clearinghouse Day!" *(56)*

NEWMAN: Kramer's pal has a keen eye for Elaine's nipple

◆ Newman falls asleep watching the Yankees game that airs opposite *Jerry (61)*

Nice Game, Pretty Boy Rude remark Newman makes to Keith Hernandez, instigating the legendary June 14, 1987, spitting incident *(34)*

Nick at Nite Rerun-jammed cable network that Elaine complains is Jerry's sole interest *(47)*

Nip Teasing nickname Elaine's office-mates give her after her nipple unexpectedly appears on the Christmas card portrait Kramer takes of her *(51)*

Nose Job Cosmetic surgery George encourages his nasally well-endowed girlfriend to undergo; the first operation is a disaster, but the second one's a beaut *(26)*
◆ Jerry explains to Elaine why he objects to boob jobs, but not nose jobs: "You don't unhook anything to get to the nose. And no man ever tried to look up a woman's nostrils." *(57)*

NICE GAME, PRETTY BOY: Did Newman's comment make Hernandez spitting mad?

Nostril Penetration Criterion Jerry and George use to determine if someone can fairly be categorized as a nose-picker *(51)*

Nothing Reason Jerry objects to Levi's Dockers ads: "They're talking about nothing!" *(9)*
◆ Ground-breakingly nihilistic nonconcept George devises (and later revises) for *Jerry*. "Nothing happens on the show. It's just like life." *(42)*

Nothing's Finer Than Being in Your Diner
Corny phrase Jerry scrawls on an autographed picture for a waitress; after Elaine mocks it, he asks for the picture back, and a fracas ensues *(45)*

Not That There's Anything Wrong With That Jerry and George's knee-jerk addendum to all their denials of a newspaper story alleging they are lovers; echoed by Jerry's mom, George's mom, and Kramer *(55)*

Colin O'Brien and Dylan Murphy Fake names George and Jerry adopt to finagle a free limousine ride, unaware the driver is headed for a neo-Nazi rally where George will be mistaken for an Aryan leader named Donald O'Brien *(35)*

Off the Wagon Phrase that inspires much debate when Elaine dates a recovering alcoholic; Jerry explains why an unreformed drunk is "on the wagon": "In the old days, how do you think they got the alcohol from town to town?…On a wagon!" *(29)*

One-on-One Two-person basketball game used as relationship metaphor, which Jerry refers to when Elaine says how difficult it is to talk to George when Jerry's not around: "One-on-one's a whole different game—[you] can't pass off" *(21)*
◆ George doesn't want to double-date with Jerry and Elaine; he wants to go "one-on-one" with Cheryl Fong *(53)*

Operating Theater Stadiumlike surgery room that makes Jerry nervous: "I don't want them doing anything that has other doctors saying, 'I gotta see this!'" *(6)*
◆ While observing a splenectomy from an operating theater balcony, Kramer unwisely offers Jerry a Junior Mint *(58)*

Orioles Cap Baltimore baseball-team hat that Elaine refuses to remove when she

sits in the Owners Box at Yankee Stadium on two separate occasions; she is dragged away by security guards both times *(37)*

¹Out Reason Jerry says people come to see him at comedy clubs: "Do you know why we're here? To be out." *(1)*

²Out To drag someone out of the closet; Jerry objects to a report that he is gay: "I've been outed! I wasn't even in!" *(55)*

Overdose of Odor Potential ailment Elaine ponders: "If you were locked in a vomitorium for two weeks, could you actually die from the odor?" *(28)*

Papaya King Hot dog restaurant that lures Kramer away from a movie theater where he is waiting to meet Jerry *(52)*

The Panties Your Mother Laid Out for You? Jerry's non sequitur, mood-killing reply to a dirty comment a date (who happens to be Elaine's assistant) makes about her panties; she repeats Jerry's remark to Elaine, who teases him about it *(46)*

Papier-Mâché Hats Objets d'art created by a pretentious girlfriend of George's, which cannot be worn in the rain *(19)*

Pasta Primavera Italian vegetable and noodle dish NBC president Russell Dalrymple orders at a fancy restaurant and Elaine sneezes on; Russell suffers intense gastric discomfort as a result *(54)*

ORIOLES CAP: Don't try to make Elaine forsake her hometown team

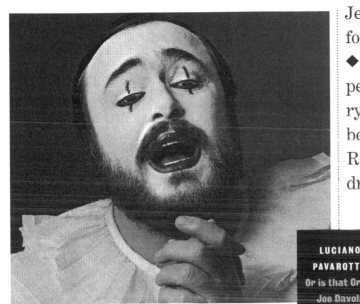

Luciano Pavarotti Italian tenor performing the role of Pagliacci, the tragic clown, when Crazy Joe Davola terrorizes Jerry and Elaine at the opera house *(47)*

LUCIANO PAVAROTTI: Or is that Crazy Joe Davola behind the greasepaint?

Pear Piece of fruit Jerry and George bicker over the cleanliness of in front of a reporter, adding to her impression that they are romantically involved *(55)*

Peek Surreptitious glance Kramer gives Jerry and George in a locker room; George admits he also "snuck a peek," but Jerry says he didn't: "There's certain information I don't want to have" *(34)*

◆ George gets caught in a "cleavage peek" when NBC president Russell Dalrymple's nubile 15-year-old daughter bends over while wearing a low-cut top; Russell subsequently peeks down Elaine's dress and falls in love *(54)*

Pen Rare NASA writing tool reluctantly given to Jerry by a neighbor of his parents; Jerry's mom makes him give it back after other condo-dwellers gossip about the transaction *(20)*

◆ George won't carry a pen in his front pants pocket for fear of stabbing his scrotum *(23)*

The Perfect Pickup George's foolproof formula for airport pickups: If he arrives 17 minutes after the plane lands, he can pull up at the precise moment when his friends are ready to hop in the car *(50)*

The Pervert in the Park With the Present in His Pants Shadowy figure from

Kramer's childhood whom he remembers while he's being grilled during the Smog Strangler case *(41)*

The Pesto of Cities George's term for Seattle—he resents the sudden trendiness of both the basil sauce and the Northwest city *(17)*

Pez Dispenser Difficult-to-load cartoon candy holder that Jerry places on Elaine's leg during a classical piano recital, causing her to burst out laughing *(31)*

Phase Two Jerry's phrase for the second stage of a relationship, marked by "extra toothbrushes, increased phone call frequency, [and] walking around naked" *(5)*

Phony Derisive adjective a friend of Kramer's uses to describe Jerry; when Jerry confronts him about it, the friend claims it's a positive word in street slang: "Man, that Michael Jordan is so *phony*." *(38)*

PEZ DISPENSER: Tweety enjoyed the concert, but not as much as Elaine

Pick Nasal no-no a model thinks she catches Jerry committing, but he insists it was just a scratch; finally, an exasperated Jerry stands up for the pickers of the world by paraphrasing *The Merchant of Venice*: "If we pick, do we not bleed?" *(51)*

[1]Ping Ominous noise Elaine claims she hears coming from Jerry's car *(17)*

[2]Ping Chinese-food deliveryman who translates George's call to a Beijing doctor who has found a baldness cure *(25)*
◆ Ping rams his bicycle into a parked car to avoid running into a jaywalking Elaine, and threatens a lawsuit *(48)*
◆ Ping's attorney cousin, Cheryl Fong, drops the lawsuit, then picks it back up again *(53)*
◆ Ping watches the pilot for *Jerry* with Cheryl *(61)*

Plan 9 From Outer Space Awful movie that Jerry wants to see with

PLAN 9 FROM OUTER SPACE: Jerry's idea of a good night out at the movies

George and Elaine in a theater, but they might miss because they're waiting for a table in a Chinese restaurant *(16)*

Polar Bear Club Group Kramer swims with in subzero temperatures; he subsequently comes up with the concept for his cologne, The Beach *(31)*

Ponce de León Biopic of the explorer that Jerry and George consider seeing instead of *Prognosis Negative*, which Elaine has asked Jerry to "save" to see with her *(21)*

◆ While waiting on line for another movie, George admits he wept during *Ponce*'s Fountain of Youth sequence, and Elaine ridicules him for it *(52)*

The Pony Remark Foot-in-mouth comment Jerry makes to an elderly cousin about how he hates people who had ponies as childhood pets; the relative says Jerry has insulted the memory of her pony, "The Pride of Krakow," and dies soon after *(7)*

The Pop-In Unexpected visit to someone's home—a pet peeve of Jerry's; Jerry is worried Elaine will be popping in all the time if she moves into his building *(10)*
◆ George admits he's a "big pop-in guy"; Jerry calls Kramer a "huge pop-in guy" *(37)*
◆ Elaine pops in on Crazy Joe Davola and discovers the full extent of his mental illness *(47)*

Post-Mousse Period of life Kramer feels he has entered after he starts controlling his wild hair with styling foam *(10)*

ANTHONY QUINN: Great actor, terrible driver, according to Jerry

Preemptive Breakup Extreme measure George takes to get "hand" in his relationship; he dumps his girlfriend before she has the chance to leave him *(31)*

Prognosis Negative Movie Jerry says he'll see with Elaine but goes to see with George, then has to see again with Elaine *(21)*
◆ Elaine uses the title to describe an ex-boyfriend's grave medical condition *(58)*
◆ A lab tells George the test results on a possible tumor came back negative, and George panics until he is told that negative is good *(61)*

The Pull-Back Evasive sexual maneuver Jerry can't believe he gets from a woman who he thinks made obscene comments into his tape recorder at a comedy club; in fact, Elaine jokingly made the tape *(25)*

The Queen Is Dead Pronouncement Jerry makes after Elaine, who has dubbed herself "Queen of the Castle," admits defeat in the contest to see who can last the longest without masturbating *(49)*

The Queen of Confrontation Title Jerry awards Elaine after she confronts a neighbor about why he stopped saying hello to her *(6)*

R

Anthony Quinn Actor whose driving Jerry discusses while trying to get a date to admit that she fled an accident scene: "Quinn says he never felt so good as when he leaves a note after smackin' into a car" *(36)*

Quitters Pessimistic pedigree of the Costanza clan, according to George: "I come from a long line of quitters…I was raised to give up" *(56)*

Quone Nonexistent word Kramer tells Jerry's mother to use in a game of Scrabble; after Jerry successfully challenges the word, Kramer claims it's a medical term—"If a patient gets difficult, you quone him" *(2)*

Quotes Stock-exchange figures George tells a sexy woman on the subway he's checking so she won't know he is looking for a job in the want ads *(30)*

RAISINS: Exhibit A in the case against Tom Pepper

Raisins Dried fruit George accuses Tom Pepper, *Jerry*'s Kramer, of stealing off a table during his audition *(61)*

Reach Polite postmeal gesture George expects from his dates—they don't have to pick up the check, but they should at least make a reach for it *(47)*

Reggae Lounge Nightclub Kramer frequents; he doesn't wash the stamp off his hand so that he can get in free the next night *(26)*

Remote Control Channel-flipping device Jerry says men use impatiently to "hunt" for shows, but women use to find a show they like and "nest" *(15)* ◆ Jerry rebukes Elaine for criticizing his remote-control technique: "How dare you impugn my clicking?" *(37)*

◆ The Bubble Boy's father lets his son keep the remote in his plastic chamber, but admits "it's frustrating" *(45)*
◆ The Bubble Boy watches *Jerry* with his parents and demands the remote to change the channel *(61)*

Roasted Potatoes Dish George's mother prepares on special occasions, like the day George promises "the surprise of a lifetime" after he finds a copy of a statue he broke as a child *(11)*

Rochelle, Rochelle Soft-core art-house film about "a young woman's strange erotic journey from Milan to Minsk," which George, Elaine, and Jerry wander into separately when they lose track of each other at a movie theater *(52)*
◆ George is returning a tape of *Rochelle, Rochelle* to a video store when he runs into Susan and her lesbian lover *(59)*

Roll-Out Tie Dispenser Disposable fashion accessory invention in which Kramer wants Jerry to invest *(5)*

REMOTE CONTROL: The Bubble Boy pushes all the wrong buttons

Rubber Man Superhero to whom Jerry compares a male maid who cleans a tiny space between the refrigerator and the counter; Jerry is surprised when Elaine informs him there is no such comic-book character as Rubber Man *(11)*

Salman Rushdie Reclusive *Satanic Verses* author Kramer swears he has seen at a health club; the Rushdie look-alike tells Kramer his name is "Sal Bass" *(57)*
◆ Sal watches *Jerry* with Sidra, the well-built woman Jerry dated *(61)*

S

Bob Sacamano Unseen friend Kramer says got butchered when he went into the hospital for routine hernia surgery *(13)*
◆ Kramer says Sacamano underwent

shock therapy once but it didn't work due to the large size of his synapses *(19)*

◆ Kramer passes out free condoms that Bob got from his factory job in Edison, N.J.; after George uses one, Kramer learns they're defective *(33)*

The Sakharov of Cable Guys Rude Russian gulag escapee and cable-TV installer whom Kramer convinces Jerry to hire for an illegal hookup *(15)*

Salsa/Seltzer Similar-sounding words George thinks must confuse

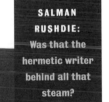

SALMAN RUSHDIE: Was that the hermetic writer behind all that steam?

Spanish people when they're ordering in restaurants *(42)*

Sauce Me Command Elaine gives her hairdresser when she can't get an odor out of her hair—she has heard that rinsing it with tomato sauce might do the trick *(59)*

Fred Savage Youthful *Wonder Years* star whom Kramer terrifies by approaching in an L.A. café and pitching a film project *(40)*

Second Button Theory Jerry's belief that the second button is the most important part of a shirt; if it's too high, "you look like you live with your mother" *(1)*

Second Spitter Theory Jerry's contention that Keith Hernandez could not have been the culprit on June 14, 1987, when Kramer and Newman were loogied upon at Shea Stadium *(34)*

See the Baby Annoying refrain Jerry hears from a couple with a newborn daughter: "Come over and *see the*

JERRY SEINFELD

◆ a.k.a. Sein *(27)*, The Sein *(61)*, Jerry Jerry Dingleberry *(58)*, Seinsmelled *(58)*, Diggity Dog *(56)*, Jerry I, the Once and Future King of Comedy *(11)*, Comedian of the United States *(47)*, and the Didja Ever Notice This/Didja Ever Notice That? Guy *(61)*

◆ Graduated from JFK High School with George in 1971 *(22)*

◆ Estimates he had sex with Elaine 25 times while they were dating *(14)*

◆ Gargles six times a day—very quietly—according to Elaine *(21)*

◆ Says he talks on the phone with George six times a day *(21)*

◆ Thinks he can tell just by looking at people whether they wear slippers (28)

◆ Proclaims proudly that he has never watched a single episode of *I Love Lucy* *(9)*

◆ Says he could read the sports section if his hair were on fire *(21)*

◆ Claims to be lactose-intolerant: "I have no patience for lactose" *(9)*

◆ Jokes that he can't eat sugar because it "makes my ankles swell up, and I can't dance" *(7)*

◆ Won't allow any soft cheeses in his refrigerator *(3)*

◆ Has never eaten "a really good pickle" *(13)*

*baby...*When are you going to *see the baby?*" *(34)*

Sic Semper Tyrannis Latin phrase meaning "Thus Always to Tyrants!" which John Wilkes Booth yelled when he assassinated Lincoln and Crazy Joe Davola repeats when he jumps Jerry *(61)*

Sidra Well-endowed woman Jerry meets at a health club and offends by inquiring about the veracity of her mammary glands *(57)*
◆ Sidra hooks up with Salman Rushdie look-alike Sal Bass *(61)*

Single, Thin, and Neat Qualities Jerry possesses that lead people to believe he might be gay *(55)*

Smog Strangler Serial killer Kramer is mistaken for while living in L.A. *(40, 41)*

Snapple Brand of drink sometimes found in Jerry's refrigerator *(48, 53)*

Sneakers Shoes George tells a girlfriend his father wears in the pool; he's trying to distract her while Jerry swipes an answering machine tape with embarrassing messages from George *(9)*
◆ First line of dialogue in *Jerry*: "New sneakers?" *(61)*

The Snub Cold-shoulder technique Kramer claims drives women mad with desire; George says he tried snubbing women for a year with no luck *(54)*

SNAPPLE: Jerry gets juiced on it

Something What Jerry knows he hears when George and Elaine mutter obscenities about him under their breath, then claim they didn't say anything *(39)*
◆ What George doesn't want *Jerry* to be about: "Everybody's doing *something*. We'll do nothing." *(42)*

Spectacular Adjective Calvin Klein uses to describe Kramer's physique *(51)*
◆ Sidra uses the word to describe her ample breasts after

she tells Jerry that they're real and she will never let him touch them *(57)*

Spector Offscreen friend of Kramer's with an eye for obese women *(23)*
◆ Kramer says Spector gave him his video camera because he's becoming a minimalist; Jerry asks, "Doesn't his fat fetish conflict with his minimalism?" *(25)*

Sponge Bath Hospital-room cleansing a sensuous female nurse gives to a curvaceous patient, distracting George from his mother's anti-onanism tirade *(49)*
◆ George tries in vain to ignore the two muscular men who perform the exact same routine while he's telling his mother he's not gay *(55)*

Joseph Stalin Soviet tyrant Jerry says he would have hung out with as a kid if Stalin would have let him use his Ping-Pong table *(4)*
◆ A Chinese doctor with a baldness cure promises George he'll grow a thick head of hair like Stalin's *(25)*

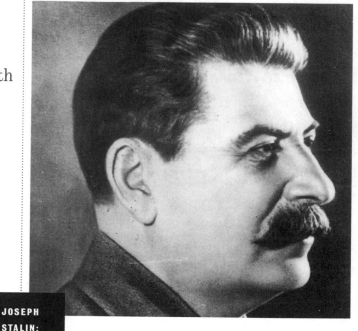

JOSEPH STALIN: George's hirsute hero, Jerry's Ping-Pong pal

Stall Men George's term for men, like himself, who don't care for urinals *(18)*

Statute of Limitations Legal phrase Kramer insists starts with "statue"; Jerry finally gives in—"Fine, it's a sculpture of limitations" *(24)*

Stella! Marlon Brando's trademark line from *A Streetcar Named Desire*, which Elaine, loopy on muscle relaxants, bellows at Jerry's Aunt Stella in Florida *(20)*

Superman Superhero who serves as a key cultural reference point for Jerry and George; Jerry wonders if Superman has a "supersense of humor," and George laments that Superman can't spin the earth backward so that Jerry can go back in time and relive a bad week *(5)*

◆ Jerry compares Kramer to Superman's archrival Lex Luthor for his ability to hatch nefarious schemes *(12)*

◆ Jerry offers to buy George a Superman comic while he's in the hospital *(13)*

◆ Jerry speculates that if baldness were eliminated in China, it would create "a nation of Supermen" *(25)*

◆ George compares Susan's father's cabin to Superman's fortress of solitude *(46)*

◆ George says Jerry's life "revolves around Superman and cereal" *(53)*

◆ Jerry is attracted to a reporter who looks like Superman's squeeze, Lois Lane *(55)*

◆ Jerry says "even Superman would be helpless" against a valet's noxious B.O. *(59)*

Susan NBC programming executive George asks out after the *Jerry* pitch meeting; Kramer vomits on Susan's suede vest, and she sends George the bill *(42)*

◆ Susan and George stop by the Bubble Boy's house on the way to her father's cabin, which Kramer burns down *(45)*

◆ Susan learns of her father's sexual exploits with John Cheever *(46)*

◆ Susan loses her job after George kisses her during an NBC meeting *(48)*

◆ George grows tired of Susan, and incites her to break up with him by picking his nose in front of her *(51)*

◆ George's attraction to Susan reawakens when he finds out she is dating a woman *(59)*

◆ Susan watches *Jerry* with a new female lover, a fellow Costanza castoff *(61)*

SUPERMAN: It's a bird, it's a plane, it's Jerry's favorite flyboy

Svengali Celebrated mesmerist to whom Elaine compares her spellbinding psychiatrist, with whom she has a whirlwind affair; she mispronounces the word as "Sven-jolly" and Jerry chides her, "Maybe he's got…a cheerful mental hold on you" *(43)*

Sweatpants Loose-fitting warm-up garment that George starts wearing; Jerry says he's sending the message to the world "I give up….I'm miserable, so I might as well be comfortable" *(61)*

T

Tampax Feminine-hygiene product; if a man lets a woman keep these in his house, Jerry says, he should officially consider her his girlfriend *(48)*

Thank You Wave Courtesy Jerry expects to receive when he lets another driver into his lane *(36)*

These Pretzels Are Making Me Thirsty Kramer's single line in a Woody Allen movie; he gets fired after one take, but his pals start using the line as an all-purpose exclamation of exasperation *(28)*
◆ Kramer tells George he "never felt so alive" as when uttering that line, so he is heading off to L.A. to pursue a movie career *(39)*

This, That, and the Other Elusive combination that prevents Jerry and Elaine from having a successful romantic relationship; *this* refers to friendship, *that* means sex, and *the other* is the intangible element they can't seem to sustain *(14)*

The Three Stooges Slapstick comedy team to whose aggressive ringleader, Moe, Jerry compares Elaine's two-

SWEATPANTS: George might as well be wearing a white flag

Tippy Toe Code words George utters to warn Jerry a woman is entering the room where Jerry is switching her phone-machine tape; they also consider singing "Lemon Tree" and "(How Do You Solve a Problem Like) Maria" *(9)*

Toe Digit that Jerry thinks, if displayed by one driver to another, could convey even greater anger than "the finger" *(3)*

◆ George suggests a joke to Jerry about how "the big toe is the captain of the toes," but if the second toe is larger, it can stage a "coup de toe"; Jerry tries the line on an audience, and it bombs *(25)*

◆ George doesn't like his bed to be made so tightly that he can't stick his toes straight up *(40)*

Toilet Paper Museum Institution that Jerry thinks should be founded to cover such topics of interest to George as "toilet paper during the Crusades, the development of perforation, [and] the first six-pack" *(42)*

THE THREE STOOGES: The comic inspiration for Kramer, George, and Jerry?

fisted writer father, Alton Benes *(8)*

◆ Jerry claims Curly died after taking the same holistic elixir that George ingests *(13)*

◆ Jerry tells a woman he's dating he will run away "like the Three Stooges at the end of every movie" if her comatose boyfriend wakes up *(32)*

◆ Kramer's Norma Desmondesque L.A. neighbor reminisces about her greatest screen role, as a secretary in a Three Stooges short *(40)*

Toothbrush Dental implement Jerry defends with the mock proclamation "I'll be damned if I'm gonna stand here and let you insult my toothbrush," after a girlfriend disses his brush's lack of bristles *(32)*

Tough Minutes 60-second increments that seem much longer than that to George while doing such things as letting a car warm up or waiting for hair conditioner to work in the shower *(17)*

Tough Monkeys Term Jerry uses to describe Elaine and himself after he makes a man cry and she says she once kicked a man in the groin to get a cab *(4)*
◆ Jerry reapplies the name to the hard-nosed library cop Bookman: "That is one tough monkey" *(22)*

Triangle Boy Jerry's contemptuous nickname for one of Elaine's ex-boyfriends, an artist who paints triangles *(58)*

Tropic of Cancer/Tropic of Capricorn Risqué Henry Miller novels Jerry checked

UNCLE LEO: He always knows what time it is, thanks to Jerry

out of the library in 1971; 20 years later, Bookman tracks him down for never returning *Cancer (22)*

Trunks Outdated word for men's swimwear; according to Jerry, "Fathers don't wear bathing suits—they wear *trunks*" *(20)*

Tuck Bed-making style George avoids because he once pulled a hamstring wrestling his way out of a too tightly tucked bed *(35)*
◆ George tells the hotel maid in L.A. that

Jerry wants a "tuck," but he prefers "no tuck," so that he can "swish…and swirl" his blankets *(40)*

Uncle Leo Jerry's arm-grabbing, ear-bending relative who bores Jerry with stories of Cousin Jeffrey *(7)*
◆ Uncle Leo notes Jerry is wearing sunglasses inside and asks, "Who are you— Van Johnson?" *(20)*
◆ Jerry upsets Uncle Leo by cutting a conversation short because he's late for a meeting at NBC *(42)*
◆ Jerry throws away a watch his parents gave him, and Uncle Leo retrieves it from the garbage *(42)*
◆ Jerry's father throws away a wal-

let Jerry gives him, and Uncle Leo fishes it out of the same garbage can *(44)*

Underwear George tells a date he owns 40 pairs of underwear and someday hopes to amass "over 360 pairs…I'll only have to do wash once a year" *(9)*
◆ George displays his severely stretched jockey shorts after having been subjected to an "Atomic Wedgie" *(22)*
◆ George admits he doesn't wear underwear sometimes because he's too lazy to do laundry; Kramer models men's briefs for Calvin Klein *(51)*

UNDERWEAR: For George, it's 40 and counting

The Unshushables Jerry's name for movie theater rowdies who refuse to quiet down under any circumstances *(10)*

Uromysitisis Poisoning Bogus ailment Jerry informs a mall security guard is the reason he had to take a leak behind a parked car *(23)*

Vacuum Cleaner Appliance Kramer lent to his neighbor Martín, who later fell into a coma; Newman offers to lend Kramer his manual carpet sweeper, but Kramer says, "The carpet sweeper is the biggest scam perpetrated on the American public since one-hour Martinizing" *(32)*

Art Vandelay Imaginary importer/exporter Jerry and George say they're visiting when they hang out in a building where a woman Jerry wants to ask out works; they also consider the names Burt Harbinson and Art Corvelay *(2)*
◆ George reuses the name when he is being interviewed by Elaine's Pendant Publishing boss and is asked what authors he likes to read; he says

VACUUM CLEANER: The only way to sweep, according to Kramer

Art Vandelay is a little-known beatnik who wrote the book *Venetian Blinds* *(29)*

Vandelay Industries Latex manufacturer George invents when asked by his unemployment officer where he has been interviewing *(34)*
◆ The company is mentioned in *Jerry* *(61)*

Martin Van Nostrand Pseudonym Kramer adopts to audition for the role of Kramer in *Jerry* *(61)*

Peter Van Nostrand Pseudonym Kramer adopts to sneak into his mother's ex-boyfriend's apartment to reclaim a jacket *(26)*

The Vault Impenetrable mental chamber where Jerry swears to keep secrets *(33)*
◆ When Jerry decides he must spill a secret that he told Kramer he would lock away, he laments, "Oy, the vault!" *(38)*

VENTRILOQUIST: How does that little dummy do it?

quist when he was a child, to his father's horror *(24)*

The Virgin Nickname for Marla, Jerry's prudish closet-organizer girlfriend, whom Elaine shocks with an anecdote about her diaphragm *(48)*
◆ Marla says she's ready to go all the way, but when Jerry tells her about the masturbation competition in which he is involved, she flees into the bed of John F. Kennedy Jr. *(49)*
◆ Marla watches *Jerry* with JFK Jr. and denounces her ex as "horrible, horrible" *(61)*

Velcro Adhesive fabric Jerry's father boasts he never used in the raincoats he made *(43)*
◆ Jerry's father throws away a wallet Jerry gives him because it's made with Velcro *(44)*

Ventriloquist Type of comic whose mannequin's kinky sex life Jerry speculates about *(22)*
◆ George says he wanted to be a ventrilo-

Volcano Relief Fund Fly-by-night charity for which Kramer collects donations during Jerry's first date with Elaine; Jerry chips in, and gets audited as a result *(19)*

Vomit Sympathy Cards Greeting cards that could be sent as an apology for upchucking on someone; Jerry imagines the inscriptions "You wear it well" and "Next time, lunch is on me" *(42)*

Robert Wagner Dashing *Hart to Hart* star whom George thinks he resembles when looking in his favorite mirror, in Monk's rest room *(3)*

..allet Money holder that Jerry's dad thinks he has lost at a doctor's office *(43)*

Jerry gives his father a new wallet with $400 slipped inside, but his father throws it away because it is made with Velcro *(44)*

◆ Elaine finds Jerry's dad's old wallet between the cushions of his couch *(61)*

..atch Lost possession of Elaine's that Jerry returns as a gift *(29)*

Uncle Leo finds and wears a

ROBERT WAGNER: Mirror, mirror on the wall...

watch that Jerry received as a gift from his parents, then threw away; Jerry finally comes clean with his folks *(42, 43, 44)*

We Have to Talk The four worst words in the English language, Jerry says; George thinks that distinction belongs to "Whose bra is this?" and Jerry concurs *(4)*

We're Living in a Society! Reminder George gives to a woman who won't get off a pay phone when George needs to make an important call *(16)*

◆ George says it again to a man with a watch who won't give him the time *(35)*

George Wendt Portly *Cheers* star whom George meets backstage at *The Tonight Show*, offering the advice "enough with the bar already"; Wendt calls George a "nut" during his on-air interview *(40)*

GEORGE WENDT: "What about a rec room or a community center?"

Wheelchair Mode of transportation utilized by Susan's partially paralyzed aunt *(46)*

◆ A woman in a wheelchair is injured after she can't park in a handicapped spot that George occupies; Kramer falls in love with the woman, but she rolls right out of his life *(60)*

The Wheels on the Bus Line from a kids' ditty on television that Jerry sings along with in order to drown out Kramer's description of a nude woman he sees in a nearby window while Jerry is attempting to abstain from masturbation *(49)*

Wipe Your Wheels Standing request Susan's mother makes of her paraplegic sister-in-law *(46)*

Wood Material of which Elaine dreams Jerry's teeth are made *(2)*
◆ Jerry considers renting an apartment with a fireplace and wonders how much one should tip a "wood guy" *(3)*
◆ George tells a woman he doesn't want to go to Hawaii because he heard the winds there blow around bits of wood and lava *(26)*
◆ Kramer says he's going to redo his entire apartment in wood *(58)*
◆ Kramer says the faux wood wallpaper makes his place feel like a ski lodge *(59)*
◆ In the NBC pilot, Jerry is puzzled when his butler says he needs more Pledge, since there is no wood in the apartment *(61)*

Wuss Supreme insult that goads Jerry and George to new levels of courage *(9, 11)*

Xiang Xao Chinese doctor whose baldness cure George learns about while watching CNN; George applies the malodorous medication, and Kramer says he spies a few new buds on George's scalp *(25)*

X-RAY COUNTER: Jerry thinks it's a laughing matter

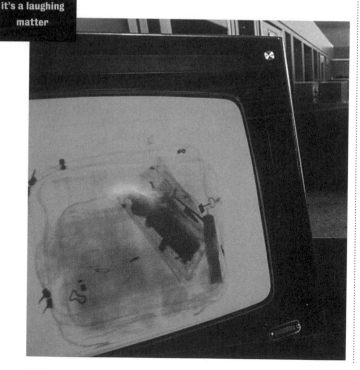

X-ray Counter Airport metal detector George sets off; Jerry then writes a joke about X-ray counters for his *Tonight Show* gig but loses it *(40)*

X-ray Room Doctor's office chamber where Jerry's father reluctantly goes without his pants; when he returns, he thinks his wallet has been "pinched" *(43)*

Yearn Verb Kramer uses to describe his deep desire to make his life meaningful; George says he craves constantly but has never yearned *(39)*

Yoo-hoo Chocolate-flavored drink that the Bubble Boy's father delivers in his truck *(45)*

You Are So Good Looking Postsneeze comment Jerry suggests as a preferable

YOUR MOTHER'S UGLIER THAN HAZEL: One maid whose allure escapes George

Your Mother's Uglier Than Hazel Childhood taunt directed at George because Mrs. Costanza was "the only mother in the neighborhood who was worse-looking than Hazel," the homely sitcom housekeeper played by Shirley Booth *(30)*

Yo-Yo Toy Jerry brings to amuse himself when he accompanies Elaine to the hospital room of one of her ex-boyfriends *(58)*

Z

alternative to the traditional "God bless you" and "Gesundheit" *(36)*

Your Mother's a Whore Parking garage demarcation Jerry thinks would be easier to remember than the standard color-letter-number system; he also proposes "My Father Is an Abusive Alcoholic" *(23)*

Zipper Jobs Type of heart surgery Kramer predicts George will have to undergo; he says doctors "love to do zipper jobs" *(13)*

Zip Up Modesty-saving maneuver George opts to make instead of catching his fainting mother when she walks in on him in the midst of a self-abuse session *(49)*

EPISODE GUIDE

THE *SEINFELD* CHRONICLES

The Seinfeld Chronicles

Original air date: July 5, 1989
Written by Larry David & Jerry Seinfeld
Directed by Art Wolff

◆ SYNOPSIS: Jerry (Jerry Seinfeld), anxiously awaiting a visit from Laura, a woman he met in Michigan, asks George (Jason Alexander) to accompany him to the airport. Jerry's romantic plans go awry when Laura mentions she's engaged. Kramer (Michael Richards) uncharacteristically knocks on Jerry's door and asks, "You up?" before entering. (Julia Louis-Dreyfus was not in the pilot. Lee Garlington played Claire, the wisecracking waitress at Pete's Luncheonette, the prototype for Monk's Cafe. Garlington did not appear again after this episode.)

◆ GUEST STAR: Pamela Brull as Laura

'MALE UNBONDING': Jerry can't shake Joel, a boyhood buddy

2 The Stakeout

Original air date: May 31, 1990
Written by Larry David & Jerry Seinfeld
Directed by Tom Cherones

◆ SYNOPSIS: Jerry meets a woman at a party but doesn't feel comfortable asking for her number because he's sitting next to his ex-girlfriend Elaine (Julia Louis-Dreyfus). Instead, he memorizes the name of the woman's law firm. Then, on his father's advice, Jerry hangs out with George in the lobby of her office building and "accidentally" runs into her.

◆ GUEST STARS: Lynn Clark as Vanessa (the lawyer), Phil Bruns as Morty Seinfeld (Jerry's dad, a role played by Barney Martin in subsequent episodes), Liz Sheridan as Helen Seinfeld (Jerry's mom)

3 The Robbery

Original air date: June 7, 1990
Written by Matt Goldman
Directed by Tom Cherones

◆ SYNOPSIS: Jerry's apartment is burglarized after Kramer lets himself in with the spare keys and neglects to lock the door behind him. Jerry considers moving to a luxurious new apartment that George shows him, but George decides he wants it too. A waitress at Monk's overhears their discussion of the apartment and takes it herself.

◆ GUEST STAR: Anita Wise as the waitress

4 Male Unbonding

Original air date: June 14, 1990
Written by Larry David & Jerry Seinfeld
Directed by Tom Cherones

◆ SYNOPSIS: Jerry tries to end his friendship with Joel, an annoying childhood buddy, but finds that it is impossible to "break up" with a guy. Kramer announces his plan for a chain of make-your-own-pizza restaurants.

◆ GUEST STAR: Kevin Dunn as Joel

5 The Stock Tip

Original air date: June 21, 1990
Written by Larry David & Jerry Seinfeld
Directed by Tom Cherones

◆ SYNOPSIS: George persuades Jerry to invest in a company that has developed a new technique for televising opera. The stock plummets. Jerry sells his shares, but George hangs on and ends up making a bundle. Jerry spends a disastrous weekend in Vermont with his new girlfriend, Vanessa.

◆ GUEST STAR: Lynn Clark as Vanessa

6 The Ex-Girlfriend

Original air date: January 23, 1991
Written by Larry David & Jerry Seinfeld
Directed by Tom Cherones

◆ SYNOPSIS: George breaks up with Marlene, a sexy Southern belle, but remembers he left some books at her apartment. When Jerry retrieves the books, he finds himself attracted to Marlene. Marlene and Jerry start dating, but she quickly drops him because she doesn't think his stand-up act is funny.

◆ GUEST STAR: Tracy Kolis as Marlene

7 The Pony Remark

Original air date: January 30, 1991
Written by Larry David & Jerry Seinfeld
Directed by Tom Cherones

◆ SYNOPSIS: At a family gathering, Jerry offends an elderly cousin, Manya, with an offhand comment about his hatred for kids who had ponies when they were growing up. After defending the memory of her childhood pet, Manya dies. Jerry wonders if he's responsible.

◆ GUEST STARS: Rozsika Halmos as Manya, Barney Martin as Morty Seinfeld, Liz Sheridan as Helen Seinfeld, Len Lesser as Jerry's Uncle Leo

8 The Jacket

Original air date: February 6, 1991
Written by Larry David & Jerry Seinfeld
Directed by Tom Cherones
◆ SYNOPSIS: Jerry buys an expensive suede jacket and wears it out to dinner with Alton Benes, Elaine's cranky novelist father, whom Jerry and George must entertain when Elaine doesn't show up on time. Jerry ruins his jacket by wearing it in a snowstorm.
◆ GUEST STAR: Lawrence Tierney as Alton Benes

9 The Phone Message

Original air date: February 13, 1991
Written by Larry David & Jerry Seinfeld
Directed by Tom Cherones
◆ SYNOPSIS: George leaves a series of angry messages on the answering machine of Carol, a woman he thinks is ignoring him. When she calls George from out of town, he asks Jerry to help him steal her answering-machine tape before she can hear it. After Jerry snags the tape, Carol says she has already listened to it and thinks it was just a joke.
◆ GUEST STAR: Tory Polone as Carol

10 The Apartment

Original air date: April 4, 1991
Written by Peter Mehlman
Directed by Tom Cherones
◆ SYNOPSIS: Jerry worries that his romantic style might be cramped if Elaine moves into his apartment building. The vacant pad is rented to a noisy rock band instead. George wears a wedding ring to a party because he thinks it will attract women, but it scares several potential dates away.
◆ GUEST STARS: Tony Plana as Manny (the building super), Glenn Shadix as Harold (the landlord)

11 The Statue

Original air date: April 11, 1991
Written by Larry Charles
Directed by Tom Cherones
◆ SYNOPSIS: Jerry accuses the man he hired to clean his apartment, the boyfriend of a Finnish novelist whose work Elaine wants to edit, of stealing a statue once owned by Jerry's grandfather. Kramer poses as a cop and forces his way into the man's apartment to recover the statue.
◆ GUEST STARS: Michael D. Conway as Ray (the apartment cleaner), Nurit Koppel as Rava (the novelist)

12 The Revenge

Original air date: April 18, 1991
Written by Larry David
Directed by Tom Cherones
◆ SYNOPSIS: George quits his job at the real estate agency, then slips his boss a Mickey when he won't give George his job back. Meanwhile, Jerry and Kramer settle a score with a Laundromat owner who they mistakenly think ripped them off.

'THE PONY REMARK': Jerry catches heat from his parents

'THE PEN':
Elaine's in orbit during a visit to Jerry's folks in Florida

◆ GUEST STARS: Fred Applegate as Levitan (George's boss), Teri Austin as Ava (George's coworker), John Capodice as Vic (the Laundromat owner)

13 The Heart Attack

Original air date: April 25, 1991
Written by Larry Charles
Directed by Tom Cherones
◆ SYNOPSIS: George suffers what he believes is a heart attack but turns out to be tonsillitis. Elaine dates George's doctor. Kramer convinces George to visit a holistic healer, but the treatment only makes George sicker.
◆ GUEST STAR: Stephen Tobolowsky as Tor Akman (the holistic quack)

14 The Deal

Original air date: May 2, 1991
Written by Larry David
Directed by Tom Cherones
◆ SYNOPSIS: Jerry and Elaine revive their romantic relationship with a new set of ground rules: no calls allowed the day after sex, no pressure to spend the night, and no good-night kisses. Though the experiment seems to work, Jerry and Elaine have inexplicably broken up by the next episode.
◆ GUEST STAR: Siobhan Fallon as Tina (Elaine's roommate)

15 The Baby Shower

Original air date: May 16, 1991
Written by Larry Charles
Directed by Tom Cherones
◆ SYNOPSIS: Elaine hosts a baby shower in Jerry's apartment for a performance artist with whom George once had a bad date. George swears retribution, but loses his nerve. Kramer convinces Jerry to get an illegal cable-TV hookup, but when Jerry refuses to pay the steep fee, the installer smashes his TV screen.
◆ GUEST STARS: Christine Dunford as Leslie (the performance artist), Vic Polizos as Anatoly (the cable guy)

16 The Chinese Restaurant

Original air date: May 23, 1991
Written by Larry David & Jerry Seinfeld
Directed by Tom Cherones
◆ SYNOPSIS: Jerry, George, and Elaine spend the entire episode waiting for a table in a Chinese restaurant. Jerry is desperate to make it to a movie on time, George is awaiting a phone call from a girlfriend, and Elaine is starving. After they give up and leave the restaurant, their party is called.
◆ GUEST STAR: James Hong as the maître d'

17 The Busboy

Original air date: June 26, 1991
Written by Larry David & Jerry Seinfeld
Directed by Tom Cherones
◆ SYNOPSIS: George inadvertently gets an employee fired at a restaurant but learns he has saved the man's life because the eatery later exploded. Elaine is visited by a man she

liked much better when she first met him in Seattle.
◆ GUEST STARS: David Labiosa as Antonio (the fired busboy), Doug Ballard as Eddie (Elaine's suitor)

18 The Note

Original air date: September 18, 1991
Written by Larry David
Directed by Tom Cherones
◆ SYNOPSIS: Jerry, George, and Elaine get massages at a physical therapy clinic, and Jerry asks a dentist friend to write bogus notes for them to get reimbursed by insurance companies for the massages. The dentist gets busted for fraud. George questions his sexuality because he enjoyed his masseur's handiwork a little too much.
◆ GUEST STARS: Jeff Lester as Raymond (the masseur), Ralph Bruneau as Roy (the dentist)

19 The Truth

Original air date: September 25, 1991
Written by Elaine Pope
Directed by David Steinberg
◆ SYNOPSIS: George tells Patrice, his haughty accountant/artist girlfriend, what he really thinks of her, and his bluntness sends her into a mental institution. Jerry and George visit her there to retrieve Jerry's tax records. Elaine is unnerved by Kramer's wild affair with her roommate, Tina.
◆ GUEST STARS: Valerie Mahaffey as Patrice, Siobhan Fallon as Tina

20 The Pen

Original air date: October 2, 1991
Written by Larry David
Directed by Tom Cherones
◆ SYNOPSIS: Jerry and Elaine attend a banquet for Jerry's father in Florida. The Seinfelds' neighbor Jack Klompus offers Jerry a NASA pen for writing upside down. Jerry takes the pen, triggering a scandal that tears apart the condo community. Elaine wrenches her back sleeping on the Seinfelds' pull-out couch, then gets goofy on muscle relaxants.
◆ GUEST STARS: Barney Martin as Morty Seinfeld, Liz Sheridan as Helen Seinfeld, Sandy Baron as Jack Klompus, Len Lesser as Uncle Leo

21 The Dog

Original air date: October 9, 1991
Written by Larry David
Directed by Tom Cherones
◆ SYNOPSIS: Jerry sits next to Gavin Polone, a lush on an airplane who suffers a medical emergency and leaves his ill-behaved dog, Farfel, in Jerry's care. When the pooch interferes with Jerry's moviegoing plans, he threatens to take it to the pound, but Polone saves Farfel at the last minute.
◆ GUEST STARS: Joseph Maher as Gavin Polone (which happens to be the name of Larry David's agent), Tom Williams as the voice of Farfel (Yiddish for noodle)

22 The Library

Original air date: October 16, 1991
Written by Larry Charles
Directed by Joshua White
◆ SYNOPSIS: The New York Public Library tracks down Jerry to retrieve a long-overdue book, which George lost in their high-school locker room. George is shocked to see their high-school gym teacher has become a homeless man living on the library steps.
◆ GUEST STARS: Philip Baker Hall as Lt. Bookman (the library cop), Biff Yeager as Mr. Heyman (the gym teacher)

23 The Parking Garage

Original air date: October 30, 1991
Written by Larry David
Directed by Tom Cherones
◆ SYNOPSIS: Jerry, George, Elaine, and Kramer search for Kramer's lost car in a New Jersey mall garage. Kramer

is carrying an air conditioner, Elaine has two goldfish in a plastic bag, and Jerry and George are both arrested for urinating in public.

◆ GUEST STARS: David Dunard as the mall security guard, Cynthia Ettinger as Michele (a Scientologist who kicks George out of her car)

24 The Cafe

Original air date: November 6, 1991
Written by Tom Leopold
Directed by Tom Cherones

◆ SYNOPSIS: Jerry befriends Babu Bhatt, a Pakistani restaurateur, but his benign advice to serve only Pakistani cuisine ends up putting Babu out of business. George's girlfriend Monica asks him to take an IQ test, and George asks Elaine to take it for him. When Monica uncovers the hoax, she ditches George.

◆ GUEST STARS: Brian George as Babu Bhatt, Dawn Arnemann as Monica

25 The Tape

Original air date: November 13, 1991
Written by Larry David and Bob Shaw & Don McEnery
Directed by David Steinberg

◆ SYNOPSIS: Elaine secretly leaves an X-rated message on Jerry's tape recorder at a comedy club as a joke, and George finds himself drawn to Elaine after he finds out she's the one who did it. George calls a Chinese doctor who has discovered a cure for baldness, and asks Ping, a Chinese-food deliveryman, to translate.

◆ GUEST STAR: Ping Wu as Ping

26 The Nose Job

Original air date: November 20, 1991
Written by Peter Mehlman
Directed by Tom Cherones

'THE CAFE':
Jerry lends a not-so-helping hand to his new friend Babu

◆ SYNOPSIS: George tries to see his way past his girlfriend Audrey's one flaw—a prominent proboscis. They break up, and a surgically corrected Audrey winds up dating Kramer. Kramer cons his way into his mother's ex-boyfriend's apartment to get an adored jacket. Jerry struggles to overcome his carnal desire for Isabel, an air-headed struggling actress.

◆ GUEST STARS: Susan Diol as Audrey, Tawny Kitaen as Isabel

27 The Stranded

Original air date: November 27, 1991
Written by Larry David & Jerry Seinfeld and Matt Goldman
Directed by Tom Cherones

◆ SYNOPSIS: Jerry and Elaine tag along with George to a party on Long Island and are left without a ride home after George gets lucky with Ava, a woman from his office. The party's host, Steve, later pops by Jerry's apartment and gets plastered with Kramer. George gets busted for shoplifting while trying to get even with a drugstore clerk he thinks overcharged him.

◆ GUEST STARS: Teri Austin as Ava, Michael Chiklis as Steve

28 The Alternate Side

Original air date: December 4, 1991
Written by Larry David and Bill Masters
Directed by Tom Cherones

◆ SYNOPSIS: George fills in for Sid, the old man who parks cars on Jerry's block, and wreaks havoc on traffic. Elaine dates 66-year-old novelist Owen March, who has a stroke while she's dumping him. Kramer lands a role in a Woody Allen movie but gets fired after one take.

◆ GUEST STARS: Jay Brooks as Sid, Edward Penn as Owen March

29 The Red Dot

Original air date: December 11, 1991
Written by Larry David
Directed by Tom Cherones

◆ SYNOPSIS: After she helps him get a job at her office, George buys Elaine a marked-down cashmere sweater for Christmas, hoping she won't spot a tiny imperfection. George loses the job for having sex with the cleaning woman on his desk. Jerry unwittingly facilitates Elaine's recovering-alcoholic boyfriend's relapse.

◆ GUEST STAR: David Naughton as Dick (the alcoholic boyfriend)

30 The Subway

Original air date: January 8, 1992
Written by Larry Charles
Directed by Tom Cherones

◆ SYNOPSIS: On separate trains, Jerry encounters an obese nude man, Elaine gets stuck in a tunnel on her way to a lesbian wedding, Kramer overhears a hot tip on a horse, and George meets an enticing woman who handcuffs him to a bed and steals his clothes.

◆ GUEST STARS: Ernie Sabella as the naked guy, Barbara Stock as the sexy stranger

31 The Pez Dispenser

Original air date: January 15, 1992
Written by Larry David
Directed by Tom Cherones

◆ SYNOPSIS: George takes Jerry and Elaine to his pianist girlfriend's recital, and Elaine disrupts the concert by guffawing loudly after Jerry plunks a Pez candy dispenser down on her leg. Jerry tries to help a comic with a drug problem.

◆ GUEST STARS: Elizabeth Morehead as Noel (the pianist), Chris Barnes as Richie (the comic)

32 The Suicide

Original air date: January 29, 1992
Written by Tom Leopold
Directed by Tom Cherones

◆ SYNOPSIS: Jerry dates Gina, his neighbor Martín's girlfriend, while Martín is in a post–suicide attempt coma. Elaine fasts before an ulcer test. George gives Kramer his ticket to the Cayman Islands after a psychic warns him of impending danger, and Kramer returns with reports of his nude backgammon game with swimsuit model Elle Macpherson.

◆ GUEST STARS: Gina Gallego as Gina, C.E. Grimes as Martín, Mimi Lieber as Rula (the psychic), Wayne Knight as Newman (Jerry and Kramer's nosy neighbor)

33 The Fix-Up

Original air date: February 5, 1992
Written by Elaine Pope & Larry Charles
Directed by Tom Cherones

◆ SYNOPSIS: Jerry convinces George to go out with Cynthia, a bulimic friend of Elaine's, and Jerry and Elaine make a pact to tell each other everything their friends tell them about the date. When George and Cynthia report they slept together on the first date (using a faulty condom provided by Kramer), Jerry and Elaine clam up.

◆ GUEST STAR: Maggie Jakobson as Cynthia

34 The Boyfriend (one-hour episode)

Original air date: February 12, 1992
Written by Larry David and Larry Levin
Directed by Tom Cherones

◆ SYNOPSIS: Jerry meets former New York Met Keith Hernandez, who asks Elaine out on a date. Kramer and Newman accuse Hernandez of having spat on them five years earlier, but the real offender is revealed to be ex-Met Roger McDowell. In an attempt to get his benefits extended, George dates his unemployment officer's plain daughter. Jerry and Kramer visit a married couple's baby.

◆ GUEST STARS: Keith Hernandez and Roger McDowell as themselves, Wayne Knight as Newman

35 The Limo

Original air date: February 26, 1992
Teleplay by Larry Charles
Story by Marc Jaffe
Directed by Tom Cherones

◆ SYNOPSIS: George's car breaks down on his way to pick up Jerry at the airport, so the two hop into an unoccupied limo and end up having to pose as neo-Nazis on their way to a rally. George thinks Eva, one of the fascists, is cute. George tries to prove his real identity to protesters and TV news crews.

◆ GUEST STARS: Peter Krause as Tim (he-Nazi), Suzanne Snyder as Eva (she-Nazi), Jodi Baskerville as herself (New York City TV reporter)

36 The Good Samaritan

Original air date: March 4, 1992
Written by Peter Mehlman
Directed by Jason Alexander

◆ SYNOPSIS: Jerry follows a hit-and-run driver who turns out to be a gorgeous woman whom he asks out on a date. George has an affair with a married friend of Elaine's who has a jealous husband. Kramer's date with neighbor Becky Gelke gets off to a bad start when Mary Hart's voice causes him to have a seizure.

◆ GUEST STARS: Melinda McGraw as Angela (the dangerous driver), Helen Slater as Becky Gelke

37 The Letter

Original air date: March 25, 1992
Written by Larry David
Directed by Tom Cherones

◆ SYNOPSIS: Jerry receives a plagiarized letter from Nina, an ex-girlfriend who has painted a portrait of Kramer, and confronts her. Elaine gets tossed out of Yankee Stadium twice for wearing an Orioles cap while sitting in the Owners Box.

◆ GUEST STARS: Catherine Keener as Nina

38 The Parking Space

Original air date: April 22, 1992
Written by Larry David and Greg Daniels
Directed by Tom Cherones

◆ SYNOPSIS: George gets into a street-side scuffle with Mike, a friend of Kramer's, after he simultaneously pulls into a parking spot that George is approaching from the opposite direction. Elaine invents a farfetched story to try to convince Jerry that it's not her fault his car has been damaged.

◆ GUEST STARS: Lee Arenberg as Mike, Jay Brooks as Sid (the car-parker on Jerry's block), Wayne Knight as Newman

39 The Keys

Original air date: May 6, 1992
Written by Larry Charles
Directed by Tom Cherones

◆ SYNOPSIS: Jerry demands his spare keys back from Kramer, who has been using them constantly to let himself into Jerry's apartment. Sore at Jerry, Kramer takes off for L.A. to pursue an acting career and does a cameo on *Murphy Brown*, the CBS sitcom for which Elaine has been trying to write a script.

◆ GUEST STARS: Candice Bergen as Murphy Brown, Wayne Knight as Newman

40 The Trip, Part I

Original air date: August 12, 1992
Written by Larry Charles
Directed by Tom Cherones

◆ SYNOPSIS: Jerry and George travel to Los Angeles. A maid discards a napkin on which Jerry has scribbled down several jokes he wants to use, thus screwing up his appearance on *The Tonight Show* with Corbin Bernsen and George Wendt. Kramer approaches Fred Savage with a film treatment, but Kramer's Hollywood career is sidetracked when he's arrested as a serial killer.

◆ GUEST STARS: Fred Savage, Corbin Bernsen, George Wendt, and Keith Morrison (Los Angeles TV reporter) as themselves

41 The Trip, Part II

Original air date: August 19, 1992
Written by Larry Charles
Directed by Tom Cherones

'THE TRIP, PART II': Jerry, Kramer, and George's big adventure

◆ SYNOPSIS: Jerry and George manage to convince the L.A. police that Kramer isn't "The Smog Strangler," but in the process they mistakenly let the real killer escape from the backseat of a cop car.

◆ GUEST STARS: Clint Howard as Tobias (the killer), Keith Morrison as himself

42 The Pitch/The Ticket (one-hour episode)

Original air date: September 16, 1992
Written by Larry David
Directed by Tom Cherones

◆ SYNOPSIS: Jerry and George successfully pitch their idea for a sitcom about "nothing" to NBC. George starts dating Susan, an NBC executive on whom Kramer later vomits. Late for the NBC meeting, Jerry unwittingly offends his Uncle Leo by cutting him off in mid-anecdote. Crazy Joe Davola turns his wrath on Kramer for not inviting him to a party. Elaine vacations in Europe with her shrink, Dr. Reston. Newman enlists Kramer's aid in his futile quest to beat a speeding ticket.

◆ GUEST STARS: Bob Balaban as Russell Dalrymple (NBC president), Heidi Swedberg as Susan, Len Lesser as Uncle Leo, Peter Crombie as Crazy Joe Davola, Stephen McHattie as Dr. Reston, Wayne Knight as Newman

43 The Wallet

Original air date: September 23, 1992
Written by Larry David
Directed by Tom Cherones

◆ SYNOPSIS: Jerry's parents visit from Florida, and his father accuses a back doctor of swiping his wallet. Elaine tries to break Dr. Reston's romantic spell over her. Uncle Leo shows up at dinner wearing a watch Jerry got as a gift from his parents and later threw in a garbage can.

◆ GUEST STARS: Barney Martin as Morty Seinfeld, Liz Sheridan as Helen Seinfeld, Stephen McHattie as Dr. Reston, Len Lesser as Uncle Leo, Heidi Swedberg as Susan

44 The Watch

Original air date: September 30, 1992
Written by Larry David
Directed by Tom Cherones

◆ SYNOPSIS: Jerry offers to buy his watch back from Uncle Leo, then comes clean with his parents. George plays hardball in his negotiations with NBC and gets less money. Jerry asks out Naomi, a hostess with a horrible laugh. While Kramer is in Dr. Reston's office pretending to be Elaine's lover, Elaine meets Crazy Joe Davola. Jerry gives his father a new wallet, only to have his dad throw it away.

◆ GUEST STARS: Len Lesser as Uncle Leo, Barney Martin as Morty Seinfeld, Liz Sheridan as Helen Seinfeld, Heidi Swedberg as Susan, Bob Balaban as Russell Dalrymple, Jessica Lundy as Naomi, Stephen McHattie as Dr. Reston, Peter Crombie as Crazy Joe Davola

45 The Bubble Boy

Original air date: October 7, 1992
Written by Larry David & Larry Charles
Directed by Tom Cherones

◆ SYNOPSIS: On their way to Susan's family cabin, George and Susan's visit to a fan of Jerry's who lives in a plastic bubble turns ugly. Jerry gets into a scrape with a waitress over his autographed picture. Kramer and Jerry's ex-girlfriend Naomi make a surprise trip to the cabin, which Kramer incinerates with a cigar.

◆ GUEST STARS: Heidi Swedberg as Susan, Jon Hayman as the voice of Donald (the Bubble Boy), Brian Doyle-Murray as Mel (the Bubble Boy's father), Jessica Lundy as Naomi

46 The Cheever Letters

Original air date: October 28, 1992
Teleplay by Larry David
Story by Larry David and Elaine Pope & Tom Leopold
Directed by Tom Cherones

◆ SYNOPSIS: George and Susan tell her father about what happened to his cherished cabin, and her father's love affair with the late novelist John Cheever is revealed. Kramer bargains with Cuban government officials for more cigars. Jerry utters an embarrassing boudoir remark to Sandra, Elaine's secretary.

◆ GUEST STARS: Heidi Swedberg as Susan, Warren Frost as Susan's father, Grace Zabriskie as Susan's mother, Lisa Malkiewicz as Sandra

47 The Opera

Original air date: November 4, 1992
Written by Larry Charles
Directed by Tom Cherones

◆ SYNOPSIS: Elaine dumps Crazy Joe Davola, who dresses up as a clown and pursues her when she goes to the opera with Jerry. George and Kramer try to sell their extra opera tickets for a profit. George has a run-in with the father of a friend whose wedding George once marred with a terrible toast.

◆ GUEST STARS: Peter Crombie as Crazy Joe Davola, Gerrit Graham as First Clown (a street performer), Glen Chin as "Harry Fong" (the ticket buyer), Heidi Swedberg as Susan

'THE BUBBLE BOY': Mel tells Jerry his son is a huge fan

48 The Virgin

Original air date: November 11, 1992
Teleplay by Peter Mehlman and Peter Farrelly & Bob Farrelly
Directed by Tom Cherones
◆ SYNOPSIS: Jerry dates Marla, a sexually inexperienced closet organizer. Elaine discusses her diaphragm, which shocks Marla. George gets Susan fired by kissing her in front of Rita, an NBC superior. Elaine's jaywalking causes Ping to have a bicycle accident.
◆ GUEST STARS: Jane Leeves as Marla, Heidi Swedberg as Susan, Anne Twomey as Rita, Ping Wu as Ping

49 The Contest

Original air date: November 18, 1992
Written by Larry David
Directed by Tom Cherones
◆ SYNOPSIS: George's mother catches him masturbating. A competition to see who can forgo self abuse longest is complicated by Jerry's sex-free relationship with Marla, Elaine's flirtation with John F. Kennedy Jr., and a female nudist across the street. Kramer drops out first, followed by Elaine. Jerry and George succumb simultaneously. Disgusted by the whole affair, Marla leaves Jerry for JFK Jr.
◆ GUEST STARS: Estelle Harris as Estelle Costanza (George's mother), Jane Leeves as Marla

50 The Airport

Original air date: November 25, 1992
Written by Larry Charles
Directed by Tom Cherones
◆ SYNOPSIS: Flying home from St. Louis, Jerry enjoys a first-class seat next to model Tia Van Camp, while Elaine sits in coach with a snoring man's head on her shoulder. Kramer and George go airport-hopping to meet Jerry and Elaine's plane. Kramer accosts an ex-roommate who owes him money.

◆ GUEST STARS: Jennifer Campbell as Tia Van Camp, Jim J. Bullock as a flight attendant

51 The Pick

Original air date: December 16, 1992
Teleplay by Larry David
Story by Larry David and Marc Jaffe
Directed by Tom Cherones
◆ SYNOPSIS: Tia ditches Jerry after she thinks she has spied him picking his nose at a traffic light. George allows Susan to catch him picking his nose so that she will break up with him. Kramer's career as an underwear model is launched by Calvin Klein. Elaine accidentally exposes herself on her Christmas card. George has his first therapy session.
◆ GUEST STARS: Jennifer Campbell as Tia Van Camp, Heidi Swedberg as Susan, Nicholas Hormann as Calvin Klein, Gina Hecht as Dana (George's therapist), Wayne Knight as Newman

52 The Movie

Original air date: January 6, 1993
Written by Steve Skrovan & Bill Masters & Jon Hayman
Directed by Tom Cherones
◆ SYNOPSIS: The gang's plan to meet for a movie is confounded by Jerry's crosstown comedy club gigs, Kramer's hot dog craving, George's repeated tussles with an usher, and Elaine's inability to save seats.
◆ GUEST STAR: Barry Diamond as Buckles (a lame comic)

53 The Visa

Original air date: January 27, 1993
Written by Peter Mehlman
Directed by Tom Cherones
◆ SYNOPSIS: George romances Cheryl Fong, a lawyer who offers to help Babu, an immigrant friend whose visa extension Jerry has unintentionally delayed. Cheryl also persuades her cousin Ping to drop his lawsuit against Elaine. But

Cheryl changes her mind when she learns George asked Jerry not to be funny in front of her. A deported Babu declares his desire to exact retribution against Jerry.
◆ GUEST STARS: Maggie Han as Cheryl Fong, Brian George as Babu, Ping Wu as Ping

54 The Shoes

Original air date: February 4, 1993
Written by Larry David and Jerry Seinfeld
Directed by Tom Cherones
◆ SYNOPSIS: Elaine is enraged by Jerry's ex-girlfriend Gail's casual comment about Elaine's expensive footwear. George nearly screws up the NBC deal by ogling Russell Dalrymple's teen daughter, Molly. Russell becomes infatuated with Elaine after peering at her cleavage.
◆ GUEST STARS: Anita Barone as Gail, Bob Balaban as Russell Dalrymple, Denise Lee Richards as Molly Dalrymple, Gina Hecht as Dana (George's therapist)

55 The Outing

Original air date: February 11, 1993
Written by Larry Charles
Directed by Tom Cherones
◆ SYNOPSIS: NYU student reporter Sharon Leonard overhears a conversation in which Elaine jokes that Jerry and George are lovers. Jerry struggles to rectify this impression after Leonard writes a story "outing" them. George unsuccessfully tries to use the article to scare off his clinging girlfriend, Allison.
◆ GUEST STARS: Paula Marshall as Sharon, Kari Coleman as Allison, Estelle Harris as Estelle Costanza, Barney Martin as Morty Seinfeld, Liz Sheridan as Helen Seinfeld

56 The Old Man

Original air date: February 18, 1993
Teleplay by Larry Charles
Story by Bruce Kirschbaum

Directed by Tom Cherones
◆ SYNOPSIS: Jerry, Elaine, and George volunteer to visit senior citizens. Jerry can't stand Sid Fields, his crotchety assignee. Elaine is repulsed by the goiter on the neck of her new friend, Mrs. Oliver. George's charge, Ben Cantwell, has no time for George's obsession with death. Kramer and Newman try to get rich selling Sid Fields' record collection. George seduces Fields' Senegalese maid.
◆ GUEST STARS: Bill Erwin as Sid Fields, Edie McClurg as the voice of Mrs. Oliver, Robert Donley as Ben Cantwell, Wayne Knight as Newman, Tobin Bell as Ron (the record store clerk), Lanei Chapman as the maid

57 The Implant

Original air date: February 25, 1993
Written by Peter Mehlman
Directed by Tom Cherones
◆ SYNOPSIS: Elaine insists Jerry's pneumatic new girlfriend, Sidra, has silicone-enhanced breasts. As Sidra dumps Jerry, she tauntingly tells him she's the real thing. Kramer tries to convince Jerry that he has seen novelist Salman Rushdie at the health club. George's table manners cause an uproar at the funeral of his girlfriend Betsy's aunt.
◆ GUEST STARS: Teri Hatcher as Sidra, Tony Amendola as "Sal Bass" (Rushdie), Megan Mullally as Betsy

58 The Junior Mint

Original air date: March 18, 1993
Written by Andy Robin
Directed by Tom Cherones
◆ SYNOPSIS: Jerry and Kramer fumble with a piece of candy and end up performing an unexpected assist as they observe Elaine's ex-boyfriend Roy's splenectomy from the operating room balcony. Jerry racks his brain to remember the name of the woman he's dating, but she walks out on him before he can come up with it.
◆ GUEST STARS: Sherman Howard as Roy, Susan Walters as Mystery Woman